978 1848428492

WHISKY GALORE

adapted for the stage by

Philip Goulding

from the novel by

Compton Mackenzie

NICK HERN BOOKS

London

www.nickhernbooks.co.uk

A Nick Hern Book

This adaptation of *Whisky Galore* first published as a paperback original in Great Britain in 2019 by Nick Hern Books Limited, The Glasshouse, 49a Goldhawk Road, London W12 8QP

Play copyright © 2019 Philip Goulding
Novel copyright © 1947 The Estate of Compton Mackenzie
Music copyright © 2019 Alan Edward Williams

Philip Goulding has asserted his right to be identified as the author of this adaptation

Cover photograph (left to right): Shuna Snow as Captain Headley-Faversham, Isabel Ford as Robbie Baird, and Joey Parsad as Joseph Macroon in the original 2018 production of *Whisky Galore*. Photo by Joel Chester Fildes.

Designed and typeset by Nick Hern Books, London
Printed in Great Britain by Mimeo Ltd, Huntingdon, Cambridgeshire PE29 6XX

A CIP catalogue record for this book is available from the British Library

ISBN   978 1 84842 849 2

Woodland
CARB N
www.woodlandcarbon.co.uk
NICK HERN BOOKS
Printed on Carbon Captured paper

COMPTON MACKENZIE

Compton Mackenzie was born in West Hartlepool in 1883. He
was educated at St Paul's School and Magdalen College,
Oxford. During the First World War he became a Captain in the
Royal Marines, becoming Director of the Aegean Intelligence
Service. He wrote more than ninety books – novels, history and
biography, essays and criticism, children's stories and verse,
and was also an outstanding broadcaster. He is perhaps best
known for the comic novels *Whisky Galore* and *The Monarch of
the Glen*. He founded and edited until 1961 the magazine
Gramophone, and was President of the Siamese Cat Club. He
lived for many years on the island of Barra in the Outer
Hebrides, but later settled in Edinburgh. Compton Mackenzie
died in 1972.

PHILIP GOULDING

Philip Goulding's stage plays include *A Fine Bright Day Today*
(Oldham Coliseum Theatre, 2011; New Vic Theatre, Stoke,
2012), *Wake Up Little Suzie!* (Oldham Coliseum/Haymarket
Theatre Basingstoke), *The Belle of Bonavista Bay* (Theatre
Newfoundland Labrador), *Beneath the Waves* (Eastern
Angles/Colchester Mercury Theatre), *Then He Kissed Me*
(Royal Theatre Northampton), *Went Down to the Crossroads*
(Courtyard Theatre, London), *Waiting for Elvis* (New
Perspectives), *Heading West* (Forest Forge/Salisbury
Playhouse), *Different Animal* (Hen and Chickens, London), *Doc
Faust! – A Wild West Musical* (Maine Performing Arts Festival),
Feels Like the First Time (Oldham Coliseum), *Horse or River?*
(Oldham Race Equality Partnership), *Czechmate* (Stephen
Joseph Theatre, Scarborough) and *Our Gracie* (Oldham
Coliseum/New Vic Stoke). His play *Strange Lands* won first
…heatre Institute Playwriting

Competition 2002 and was produced by Public View Theatre Company and Giorgos Gikapeppas at the Empros Theatre, Athens, in 2003 and premiered in the UK by N1 Theatre Company at the Courtyard Theatre, London, in 2005.

His other adaptations include *The Titfield Thunderbolt* (New Perspectives, 1997; Third Space Farnham, 2004; Bill Kenwright/Queen's Theatre Hornchurch/Windsor Theatre Royal, 2005; Bruce James Productions, 2010; Suffolk Summer Theatres, 2014), a new version of Gogol's *The Government Inspector* (Forest Forge/Salisbury Playhouse, 1997; Watermill Theatre, 1998, and as *A Little Local Difficulty* at Oldham Coliseum, 2003 and Courtyard Theatre, London, 2014), *The Road to Nab End* (Oldham Coliseum), *Toad of Toad Hall* (Alberta Theatre Projects), *The Wind in the Willows* (Basingstoke Haymarket), *Beauty and the Beast*, *Alice in Wonderland*, *Briar Rose*, *Peter Pan* and *The True Tales of Robin Hood* (all Forest Forge), *The Mayor of Casterbridge* (Forest Forge/Salisbury Playhouse, 1998; Wessex Actors Company, 2005) and, with playwright Richard Hurford, the community play *The Beggar's Opera Through the Ages* (York Theatre Royal, 2016).

For television he has written *Keeper* (Channel 4). He was a co-writer of the BBC documentary *Deadliest Crash: the Le Mans 1955 Disaster* (Bigger Picture Films).

For radio he has written *Unexpected Vonnegut*, an adaptation of Kurt Vonnegut's short story *Who Am I This Time?* for BBC Radio 4, and *A Fat Man Eats the Moon* and *The Dilemma* for RTE (Dublin).

He has collaborated on a series of projects with composer Alan Edward Williams, writing the texts for *12 Storeys High*, a song cycle for soprano and solo piano (Zoe Milton-Brown/Gavin Wayte, Bridgewater Hall/Royal Exchange, Manchester, 2010), *Divers Winged Creatures*, an award-winning choral song sequence (MDR Rundfunkchor, Leipzig 2008), *Wonder: a Scientific Oratorio* (BBC Philharmonic/BBC Singers/Salford Choral Society 2009), and the chamber opera *Stefan & Lotte in Paradise* (MediaCity 2012).

For more information, please visit www.philipgoulding.com

Introduction

Philip Goulding

Compton Mackenzie, or 'Monty' as he was known to his
friends, was born into a theatrical family. His grandfather was
Henry Compton, an actor best known for his Shakespearean
comedy roles, including the Gravedigger, which he played at
the Lyceum to Henry Irving's Hamlet in 1875. A critic wrote,
'In every scene but one [Irving] was the centre of attention, but
in that one scene in which he came to dialogue with the
gravedigger, Mr Compton, he fell immediately and naturally
into second place.'

Monty's parents were the touring players Edward Compton and
Virginia Bateman, who ran the Compton Comedy Company.
One of Monty's sisters was Fay Compton, a highly respected
classical actress in the UK, while his brother was Francis
Compton, who built a successful film and theatre acting career
in the United States.

And Monty also trod the boards himself. In fact, after the actor-
manager Arthur Bourchier saw him in a production of *The
Merchant of Venice* at Oxford University, Monty was offered
a contract as the young lead at the Garrick, on a salary rising to
the tidy sum of £2,000 per year. He turned it down – having
deduced that acting was a shallow skill. He'd decided instead to
become a writer.

In the foreword to his novel *A Passionate Elopement* – finally
published after eleven rejections – Compton Mackenzie wrote:

> I never intended to be a novelist; I always meant to be a
> playwright. In 1906, being at the time just twenty-three, I
> wrote an eighteenth-century comedy to encourage my father
> to continue the allowance of £150 a year he was then making
> me. He agreed to put *The Gentleman in Grey* (as the play was
> called) into his repertory, beginning at the Lyceum Theatre,

Edinburgh, in March 1907. The play was generously received – yet I was dissatisfied. The actors and the actresses all gave good performances, but they were none of them my characters as I had imagined them, and although *The Gentleman in Grey* remained in my father's repertory for three or four years I never saw a performance that did satisfy me.

Fortunately, his career as a novelist took off, and he went on to write over a hundred books – a few of them featuring theatrical characters, settings and themes.

Girls Will Be Boys

Shortly before being commissioned to adapt *Whisky Galore*, I'd been reading about the various touring theatre companies of the mid-twentieth century, including the Compass Players, the Adelphi Players, and the Osiris Players – Nancy Hewins' all-female company that toured the country between 1927 and 1963. I remembered having come across the Osiris Players before, and after a few hours in the attic ploughing through box-files of old newspaper cuttings, I dug out Paul Barker's 1995 *Independent on Sunday* article: *A Woman of Some Importance*. Re-reading the piece, I wondered if it would be possible to pay tribute to the spirit of Nancy Hewins in my version of *Whisky Galore*. Serendipitously, our show was scheduled to go on the road in 2018, the year Britain marked one hundred years since (some) women first gained the right to vote.

Though Shakespeare productions formed the core of the Osiris Players' repertoire, they performed many other plays with entirely female casts, including Aimée and Philip Stuart's *Nine till Six*, A. A. Milne's *Belinda*, Jerome K. Jerome's *The Passing of the Third Floor Back*, J. M. Barrie's *Quality Street*, Noël Coward's *Blithe Spirit*, William Douglas-Home's *The Chiltern Hundreds*, Roi Cooper Megrue and Walter Hackett's *It Pays to Advertise*, Charles Hawtrey's *The Private Secretary*, Clemence Dane's *A Bill of Divorcement*, the melodramas *Sweeney Todd* and *Maria Marten*, and adaptations of *Treasure Island*, *Little Women*, *The Old Ladies*, *A Tale of Two Cities* and *Oliver Twist*.

This programming – and the fact that the other companies of the period were continually adapting and reinventing classic plays, poems and other source materials – made it easy to imagine the fictional Flora Bellerby and her Pallas Players deciding, in 1955, to adapt Compton Mackenzie's 1947 novel *Whisky Galore* for their all-female company, while being careful to retain the spirit and flavour of the original novel.

In his book *I Crossed the Minch*, the poet Louis MacNeice, after interviewing Compton Mackenzie in his house at Barra, wrote that he 'looked like Lionel Barrymore on the point of turning into a bird'. And, according to Ian Jack in the *Guardian*: 'Compton Mackenzie had a theatrical nature – he would march around in a kilt and sporran, though his paternal ancestors left Scotland in the eighteenth century.'

Given that he was such a charismatic and theatrical figure, it seemed logical that Monty should be the narrator or storyteller in the Pallas Players' adaptation of his most famous novel. And once Flora had hit upon this idea, there could be no argument as to who should assume that coveted role...

Destry Rides Again

For this stage adaptation, I returned to Compton Mackenzie's novel, rather than the 1949 Ealing film version, which excised a considerable amount of the story. Although Mackenzie was credited as co-screenwriter of the film, he was vexed by the decision to remove the religious rivalry between the inhabitants of the two islands – Little Todday (Roman Catholic) and Great Todday (Protestant). Abandoning this strand meant the elimination of one of the most engaging characters in the novel – Father Macalister, the Roman Catholic priest – with his passion for Wild West novels and his utter contempt for Paul Waggett, the bumptious commander of the Home Guard. Another result of the removal of religious division from the tale is the loss of the subplot whereby Fred Odd, the English incomer, attempts to convert from Anglicanism to Roman Catholicism for the sake of Peggy Macroon, the local lass he loves – and hopes to marry.

Whisky Galore, the novel, was, of course, inspired by a true-life event: the wrecking of the *SS Politician* off Ericksay in 1941. While researching this adaptation I was pleased to read that, when the male islanders were salvaging whisky from the ship's filthy hold, in order to prevent their clothes being stained by oil they reportedly took to wearing garments abandoned by their wives. Another example of British readiness, or perhaps eagerness, to embrace the art of cross-dressing.

If This Be Magic

Built into this adaptation is the potential for the Pallas Players to fail. They have been dealt a cruel blow with the loss of one of their most popular performers, and her replacement, Juliet, may not yet be quite up to speed. But this is not supposed to be a play that goes wrong, but one which – against all the odds – succeeds.

Quick costume changes, fake facial furniture, bicycles, bird-callers, face-packs, complicated props like piles of plates: all of these conspire to set up spills, create chaos and manufacture mayhem. But really they should be seen as challenges, rather than obstacles – devices to help tighten the teamwork and strengthen the ensemble. (Just don't use the word 'ensemble' within Flora's earshot.) The intention was to make things appear very difficult in order that, through close collaboration, great skill and endless ingenuity, it can all be made to look absolutely effortless. Therefore Juliet's achievement will seem all the greater – and the total virtuosity of the Pallas Players be almost overwhelming. That's the idea…

We seek not to mock these women and their work – this is, after all, a celebration. The Pallas Players take pride in what they do, in their craft and in the design and construction of the tools of their trade. Beards and moustaches need to attach securely yet be easily removed, and should not prevent the wearer from speaking clearly and being heard. A costume must be composed of simple, easily identifiable elements, or layers that can be donned and discarded speedily and without injury.

The set design for the shows the Osiris Players toured had to fit into two large cars. Imagination was required to recreate the settings economically and practically. Often the Osiris Players would be touring more than one show at a time. During the war, Hewins presented 1,534 performances of thirty-three plays (sixteen penned by Shakespeare, the rest by lesser authors). And the set-ups and get-outs – as with small-scale touring shows on the road today – would have been managed by the performers. As Paul Barker wrote:

> They celebrated their twenty-first anniversary at a Women's Institute in Kent, with *Twelfth Night* in the morning, *Everyman* at lunchtime, *Macbeth* in the afternoon, Shaw's *Captain Brassbound's Conversion* after tea, topped off by *Badger's Green*, R. C. Sherriff's comedy about village cricket, in the evening. Not surprisingly, few of the players, outside the steady core of three or four, survived more than a couple of years with Osiris. 'We were permanently exhausted,' Susan Date remembered.

Of course, as Flora Bellerby pointed out in her unpublished autobiography *If This Be Magic*: 'A great deal of things turn out to be a lot less faff without men mucking in.' And she may have been right. But to return to Paul Barker's article:

> ...all that mattered was how it was on stage. The novelist Jane Gardam saw the Osiris Players on Teesside, where she was a child in wartime. She had never been to a play before. A van drew up outside the school, she recalls, and 'seven threadbare women got out'. They reminded her of Mr Crummles's troupe in *Nicholas Nickleby*. They looked odd, even ridiculous. She went and sat in the front row. It was *She Stoops to Conquer*. She saw 'the seven colourless women transformed into painted eighteenth-century beauties, into bumpkins and beaux, into thigh-slapping squires, into silken flirts'. They rollicked, frolicked, wept and danced their way through the play. Twelve-year-old Jane and the rest of the young audience clapped, stamped and cheered. They begged for more. Gardam never forgot these women.

It hardly needs stating that the more 'truthful' the Pallas Players' portrayals of the men in *Whisky Galore* are, the more entertaining they will be. As Flora Bellerby, again in *If This Be Magic*, advised: 'While buffoonish clowning may well amuse loved ones and immediate family, still it sells short those characters, so carefully and lovingly created that we might hold a mirror up to nature.' Or, as Alan Ayckbourn put it, rather more succinctly: 'What turns an audience off, I think, is when actors are in effect saying "Aren't I funny?"'

There's no reason, of course, why male actors shouldn't have a bash at portraying Pallas Players should they so desire. As you like it, chaps; there is, after all, some precedent in theatre history for men playing women playing men.

It's perhaps worth stressing here that this play isn't intended to be a piece 'about' all-female touring theatre companies of the twentieth century, nor is it a 'play-within-a-play'. It's an adaptation of *Whisky Galore*, as Flora Bellerby and her Pallas Players might have made, conceived as a tribute to those pioneering theatrical women, and to Compton Mackenzie – for his wit, his craft, and his imagination.

Acknowledgements

Richard Annis, Sarah Baxter, Sarah Burton, Lesley Chenery, Emma Cook, Sercha Cronin, Janet Glass, Richard Hurford, Paula Jackson, Anne-Louise Jones, Sissi Liechtenstein, Chris Monks, Brian Morton, Mary Elliott Nelson, Jill Rogers, Rose Sergent, Carl Shavitz, Kevin Shaw, Robert Teed, Kate Wilson, Liz Wilson.

P.G.

This stage adaptation of *Whisky Galore* was first presented in a co-production between Oldham Coliseum Theatre, Hull Truck Theatre and New Vic Theatre, Newcastle-under-Lyme, on 16 March 2018, with the following cast:

FLORA BELLERBY	Sally Armstrong
AILEEN McCORMACK	Lila Clements
BEA CORNFORD	Isabel Ford
JULIET MAINWARING	Alicia McKenzie
WIN HEWITT	Christine Mackie
DORIS SANDERSON	Joey Parsad
CONNIE CALVERT	Shuna Snow
Director	Kevin Shaw
Designer	Patrick Connellan
Lighting Designer	Jason Taylor
Sound Designer	Lorna Munden
Composer	Alan Edward Williams

Characters

This adaptation of Compton Mackenzie's *Whisky Galore* is being performed in a Co-op Hall in 1955 by the seven members of an all-female touring theatre company, the Pallas Players: Flora Bellerby, Connie Calvert, Win Hewitt, Doris Sanderson, Aileen McCormack, Bea Cornford and Juliet Mainwaring. Two of Mackenzie's characters – Annag and Paddy – will be played by more than one actress.

Those not 'on' at any point are to be kept busy doing whatever else is required to keep the action flowing smoothly. 'Off' is perhaps also 'on' – in that the design might allow the audience to witness the character changes, etc., as they happen.

The members of Pallas Players can hail from anywhere. The characters from *Whisky Galore* are Scottish, unless otherwise stated in the script. The suggested division of roles is as below:

FLORA BELLERBY
Monty, the author
The Biffer
Father Macalister
Constable Macrae

CONNIE CALVERT
Fred Odd
Major Quiblick
Annag No. 3
Captain Headley-Faversham

WIN HEWITT
Donald MacKechnie
Doctor Maclaren
Mrs Campbell
Annag No. 2
Tom Ferguson
Paddy No. 3

DORIS SANDERSON
Joseph Macroon
Catriona Macleod
Roderick MacRurie
Paddy No. 2

AILEEN McCORMACK
Drooby
Peggy Macroon
George Campbell
Paddy No. 1
Lieutenant Boggust/Mr Brown

BEA CORNFORD
Paul Waggett
Annag No. 1
Robbie Baird

JULIET MAINWARING
Dolly Waggett
Norman Macleod
Duncan Macroon
Annag No. 4

More detailed character descriptions are provided after the text
of the play.

Prologue

A Co-op Hall. 1955.

*Six of the Pallas Players enter while the house lights are up.
The lights dim and the women finish setting up for Act One.
They can pretend that there is a thick curtain between the actors
and the audience.*

DORIS *might discreetly look around the side of this imaginary
curtain to observe the 'house'. The atmosphere is generally
relaxed and efficient for all except* JULIET, *who double-checks
everything while studying her script.* CONNIE *calmly reads a
mechanics magazine.* AILEEN *keeps an eye on the door, acting
as lookout.* DORIS, BEA *and* WIN *make the final touches to
their preparation. Binoculars are very deliberately set.* WIN *finds
Monty's hat in the bottom of a box, whistles to* BEA, *then throws
it over to her.* BEA *places the hat. Someone whispers, 'Who's first
Perce?'*[1] *It's* JULIET, *so she tests the wooden bird-whistle. She's
a novice, so it's a bit loud. Oops. The bird-whistle is attached by
a cord to the set somewhere, to avoid it ever getting mislaid. It
probably makes only one sort of call, which has to suffice for all
the types of bird we'll encounter on our tour of the islands. At
some point* AILEEN *moves away swiftly from the door.*

AILEEN. Incoming.

Everybody looks lively. FLORA *breezes in.*

FLORA. We've a good house anyway. I've been watching
them arrive.

DORIS. What are they like?

1. When the words 'Who's Perce?' appear in the script it is a cue for the bird-
whistle. The bird-whistle is supposed to be operated by whoever is available at
that point. That person may not always remember that they are supposed to be
Perce. This may frustrate Flora. Percy Edwards (1908–1996) was an English
animal impersonator, ornithologist and entertainer.

FLORA. Anyone remember Halifax?[2]

WIN. Not really, no.

FLORA. Well, they're like that, only more so. Juliet, dear?

JULIET. Yes, Miss Bellerby?

FLORA. I'm going to do the little speech. They expect a certain standard. We can drop it once that's reached.

JULIET (*disappointed*). I understand, Miss Bellerby.

DORIS *operates curtain-winder.* FLORA *steps forward to address the audience.*

FLORA. Ladies and gentlemen. We are the Pallas Players and I am Flora Bellerby. Some of you may be aware that we have recently suffered the loss of Barbara Temple, a stalwart member of the company and one of our most popular performers, especially with some of you chaps. Barbara contracted what we first imagined was food poisoning during our week's residency at Whitehaven. As it turned out, her condition was entirely unrelated to the paucity of vitamins in Cumberland, being due instead to a rogue element picked up in Goole. Diminished as we are without Barbara's attributes, we hope all will go well for her at the Mission of Hope Maternity Hostel in Hove. Meanwhile, we're delighted to introduce, as her replacement, our enthusiastic ingénue, Miss Juliet Mainwaring.

FLORA *gestures to* JULIET, *who bows.*

Juliet only caught up with us three days hence, and has been cramming ever since, so we ask that you overlook any teething troubles, as we make-do-and-mend. Should we fall short, we hope that you'll bear with us – and as the Bard himself implored – 'Piece out our imperfections with your thoughts.' And so we give you, ladies and gentlemen, our *Whisky Galore*.

DORIS *works the Dansette. Perhaps a brief taste of Jim Cameron and his Scottish Dance Band playing 'Come Ashore Jack Tar'.*

2. This can be adapted to wherever the show is playing. If there is a 'rival' village, town or city, that should be the one used.

ACT ONE

FLORA *becomes* MONTY. CONNIE *is* FRED ODD – *English, forty-five years old.* WIN *is* DONALD MACKECHNIE.

On Board *The Island Queen*

The boat is about to dock at Snorvig, Great Todday. DONALD *on the bridge, deep in concentration.*

MONTY. A Saturday, late February, 1943. Picture the scene from the point of view of those aboard *The Island Queen* as she plies her regular route between Obaig and the Hebridian Isles. Gaze across the smooth expanse of sea to where the rugged outline of Great Todday stands dark against a mass of deepening cloud. Hark! Listen to the sea-birds call to one another...

Who's Perce?

...as we enter the Coolish, a two-mile strait separating Great Todday from its Little island neighbour. Students of literature – we may have some amongst us – will be aware that many fine tales begin with a wanderer's return. In our case the traveller takes the trim, soldierly form of Alfred Ernest Odd...

FRED *sidles in to stand beside* DONALD.

FRED. Room beside the captain for a little one?

MONTY....who never would have believed how glad he'd be to again hear the voice of Donald MacKechnie, whose small pipe was as the maiden's organ, shrill...

DONALD. Well, well, if it isn't Sergeant Odd! You've been away from us a long while this time.

FRED. Eighteen months. Peggy and me were just reckoning to get married, when they transferred me to Devonshire, then off to West Africa after that.

DONALD. Pretty annoying for you, no doubt.

FRED. That's the army. You find a job that suits, they're sure to shift you on. As you can imagine, Joseph kicked up at the idea of Peg so far away; and she wasn't keen to leave her dad. But I'm back now – and intend to get us married as soon as can be managed.

DONALD. Joseph'd struggle without Peg, for sure; she's the reliable type. (*Raises his binoculars and looks towards Snorvig pier.*) I'll say this, Sergeant, we're in for some dirty weather.

FRED. Here, I mustn't distract the man at the wheel. It's great to see you, Captain. For months I've been dreaming about these two tightest little islands in the world.

As The Island Queen *lands at Snorvig pier.*

DONALD. You'll find they're not too tight just now, Sergeant. Not too tight at all.

MONTY *steps forward. As* FLORA *speaks, she is changing from* MONTY *into* THE BIFFER. DORIS *has become* JOSEPH. AILEEN *is* DROOBY.

MONTY. Snorvig pier is crowded with familiar figures. There, in his knitted red cap, is Joseph Macroon, the Postmaster of Little Todday and Sergeant Odd's future father-in-law. And here's Drooby, whose nickname the origin of which none knows but Drooby himself, and he won't tell. Joseph and Drooby are joined on the quayside by (*Scots accent.*) The Biffer, who's sobriquet relates to his early success as a pugilist, and who these days, through rigorous study, augments his burgeoning vocabulary for the pleasure and benefit of his compatriots.

The Harbour at Snorvig

FRED *disembarks, and approaches* JOSEPH, *who distractedly shakes his hand.*

JOSEPH. Fàilte do'n dùthaich,[3] Sergeant. 'Welcome to the country', for what it's worth. (*To* DONALD.) Donald... I take it there's nothing?

DONALD. No change in the situation at all, Joseph.

FRED. I wondered would Peggy be here.

JOSEPH. Ach, she's enough to do without gallivanting about after you.

THE BIFFER *and* DROOBY *shake hands with* FRED.

THE BIFFER. It's good to see you, Sergeant.

DROOBY. Aye, it's grand to have you back.

DONALD (*to* THE BIFFER *and* DROOBY). How's Roderick, lads?

THE BIFFER. Ach, you'd barely recognise him, Donald: shrivelled almost to a carapace.

DROOBY. Pace, aye.

FRED. What on earth's the matter? Is Roderick sick?

JOSEPH. Not as such, no. But I've seldom seen the big man brought so low.

FRED. And his daughter – she's also well? Still breaking hearts up at the hotel?

THE BIFFER. Annag McRurie remains in the bloom of youth, Sergeant, never fear. I'd go so far as to proclaim her the epitome of incandescence.

DROOBY. Sense, aye. But Roderick's had a terrible time, poor soul. He said for us to come meet the boat.

---

3. *Fàilte do'n dùthaich* [fahlche don du-hich] – Welcome to the country.

THE BIFFER. We've all been hoping, Donald, how you'd be the man to lift our spirits.

DONALD. Aye, and it grieves me greatly that all I've to offer is disappointment.

DROOBY *and* THE BIFFER *console* DONALD *as all three of them head off.* AILEEN *can now swiftly become* PEGGY MACROON *while* FLORA *becomes* MONTY *again.*

FRED *realises he's still none the wiser.*

FRED. So long, boys. I suppose someone will eventually be kind enough as to put me in the picture.

JOSEPH. There's no easy way to say this, lad. There's been not a drop of whisky in the islands for twelve days. Can you credit the government letting the whisky run out so close to Lent? Before we know it there'll be no beer either. Well, Sergeant, we'll be getting across to Kiltod – so you'll be seeing Peggy in no time at all, assuming she's finished her post office chores.

The Post Office at Kiltod

MONTY. And indeed, in no time at all Joseph and Sergeant Odd traversed the short journey across the Coolish to Little Todday. There was still a glimmer of twilight when they achieved the tiny harbour at Kiltod; and there, as if to welcome back our traveller, Fred heard again the rock pipit's frail fluttering song.

Who's Perce?

Then he saw at last in the lighted door of the post office – tall and slim and beautiful as ever – his dark-haired Peggy Macroon, and a moment later they were holding hands and gazing longingly into each other's eyes.

FRED *and* PEGGY *hold hands and gaze longingly into each other's eyes.* JOSEPH *seeks to bring this unseemly display of affection to an early conclusion.*

JOSEPH. You'll be away to your bed, now, daughter of mine; the paraffin is almost empty, and you'll not want to be late for early mass.

PEGGY. It's been eighteen months, Father. I'm just so happy to have Fred back.

JOSEPH. God willing, he'll still be here tomorrow, so enough of your backchat.

PEGGY *starts to exit*. FRED *grabs her hand and brings her back to stand beside him*.

FRED (*with an air of desperation*). I was really hoping, Mr Macroon, we might settle the date when me and Peggy can get safely wed.

JOSEPH. We'll come back to that when summer's over, Sergeant. Bed, lassie, and no more about it.

PEGGY *sees that it is futile. She touches* FRED*'s face then exits*. FRED *watches her go*.

I'm sure I don't know what your hurry is, Sergeant. When the Lord made time he made plenty of it. Besides, we need to know better the way this war is going before we rush into any foolhardy decisions.

FRED. We've been wanting to marry nearly two years now. I was thinking a good time would be just before Easter.

JOSEPH. Just before Easter? You have some very peculiar thoughts.

FRED. I'm sorry, Mr Macroon, but I'm not getting any younger.

JOSEPH. Ach, it's too late to be discussing such matters. D'you know when I last had a dram, Sergeant? Twelve days ago, and Lent begins the week after next. That's a solemn sort of a time for a Catholic.

FRED. So you usually give up whisky for Lent, do you?

JOSEPH. I'm not saying that. I'll drink whisky any time of year.

FRED. We have Lent in the Church of England. I recall as a nipper having to give up sugar.

JOSEPH. Hard to imagine the English denying themselves anything. But while we're on the subject, one thing's for certain: your Mr Waggett will not be going without a dram...

MONTY *steps forward...*

MONTY. Paul Waggett was the retired London stockbroker who'd bought Snorvig House on Great Todday. He rented the shooting of the two islands from the Department of Agriculture, commanded the Home Guard, and, in the opinion of the islanders, never allowed himself to run out of creature comforts. On this occasion Joseph Macroon was right.

JULIET appears as DOLLY, *enthusiastic, pleased to have made an entrance. She carries* WAGGETT's *book.*

Just at that moment Dolly Waggett, twenty-five years married...

DOLLY *becomes less perky.*

...was concocting, for her apparently ailing husband, a hot toddy, to a recipe of his own devising.

At the mention of the 'hot toddy', JULIET *realises she's arrived sans beverage, and so has to rush off to fetch the prop. Hopefully one of the others will swiftly come to her rescue.* BEA, *as* PAUL WAGGETT, *swiftly adapts to cover the absence of* DOLLY.

Snorvig House

WAGGETT *looks out through his night-vision binoculars. He is English.*

WAGGETT. Come on, Dolly, chop chop! I detect a slight tickle, perhaps the onset of a cough; a ration of hot grog is urgently needed to fend it off. (*Focusing his binoculars.*) Well... what's this? I do believe that's old MacPhee leaving the hotel bar in high dudgeon. (*To himself.*) He's peeved, that's for sure. Dolly?!

DOLLY (*off*). Coming, dear.

JULIET *enters again as* DOLLY, *this time using the book as a tray, upon which rests* WAGGETT's *drink.* DOLLY *is English. She's wearing her dressing gown and her hair is awry.*

WAGGETT. Ah, there you are, Dolly – you took your time – I hope you're not going native, old girl; I'm still smarting over the usually reliable Sergeant Major Odd not popping in before crossing over to Kiltod. But I suppose, given his fraternisation, the wretched West Highland casualness was bound to take hold.

DOLLY. Fred's been away a long time, dear.

WAGGETT *shoots her a look.*

I'm sure the Sergeant Major was anxious to see his sweetheart again. I wonder when they'll marry?

WAGGETT. I'm more anxious to know when he'll be able to smarten up the Home Guard. The turn-out for shooting practice has been particularly poor.

DOLLY. It's disheartening for you, Paul, I'm sure, after all the trouble you've taken.

WAGGETT. When duty calls we must set aside personal feelings, Dolly.

DOLLY. Of course, dear. Now finish your drink and get to bed.

WAGGETT. You are a wise little mouse, Dolly. I shall go on up and read my book. Now where did I put it? It's a Crime Club volume: *A Corpse in the Cloisters* by Peregrine Potter.

DOLLY (*handing his book to him as they exit*). Is it a good story, dear?

WAGGETT. It doesn't scale the heights of *The Garrotted Announcer*, but it'll pass muster.

MONTY *steps forward...*

MONTY. Five miles south, at the schoolhouse in Watasett, an announcement has been made. George Campbell – the shy head of the school at Garryboo – has somehow, to everyone's astonishment including his own, persuaded bright-eyed Catriona Macleod to accept his proposal of marriage. Catriona! That splendid cook, with her deft housewifely fingers, who had just that evening served an exquisitely prepared poached pheasant for a frequent dinner guest at Watasett, popular, kind and witty Doctor Maclaren, who was firm friends and – in happier times – drinking partners with Catriona's brother Norman...

NORMAN *hasn't yet appeared.*

...the fashionably late, yet attractive young schoolmaster of Watasett: an expert poacher, ardent socialist, and confirmed bachelor.

The Schoolhouse at Watasett

GEORGE (AILEEN), DOCTOR MACLAREN (WIN) *and* CATRIONA (DORIS) *have all, where possible, acknowledged their introductions, making* NORMAN*'s absence notable.* CATRIONA *now exits, carrying a pile of plates, colliding with* JULIET, *making her late entrance as* NORMAN. *If the plates tumble, they should be unbreakable.* BEA *will move in to clear up.*

DOCTOR MACLAREN (*shouting off towards* CATRIONA). That was a splendid meal, Catriona, pleasingly augmented by the best news I've heard for ages. (*To* GEORGE.) No clue how you did it, George – but you're a lucky man for sure.

NORMAN. Aye, and while she's out of the room, George, a word to the wise. You'll have me to contend with me, mind – if you don't treat my sister right.

DOCTOR MACLAREN. Norman, George is a modest man, aye – but if Catriona has him pegged for Mr Right, we must respect her decision, however wayward it seems.

NORMAN. I'm relieved actually. Her being as good as hitched'll put my mind to rest once I join up with the RAF.

CATRIONA *re-enters.*

DOCTOR MACLAREN. There now, I'd have offered to assist with those dishes, Catriona, but I'd not seek to intercede into what'll shortly be Mr Campbell's territory. May I wish you every happiness together. And though I pray you seldom need to see me in my professional capacity, I hope to often cross your threshold as a friend you'd be happy and willing to feed. And, George – in Norman's absence you'll need to take on the role of poacher – so as to keep this kitchen goddess well supplied. And if you've to learn those dark arts on Waggett's patch, then so much the better, say I.

CATRIONA. I do wonder what your mother will think, George, when you tell her you're to be married.

NORMAN. And to a Macleod! I doubt she's even considered the notion of her wee boy tying the knot.

CATRIONA. I'm not sure she realises George is thirty-five.

NORMAN. I'm not sure she's realised he's weaned.

DOCTOR MACLAREN. Come now. I'm certain, George – once Mrs Campbell sees babies of your own clinging on to Catriona here – she'll be sure to let you go.

CATRIONA. I don't think we want to wait until after the wedding for George to sever the apron strings, doctor.

NORMAN. Ach, wouldn't everything just seem conquerable if there were whisky in the jar?

DOCTOR MACLAREN. Don't talk about it, Norman. There's not. And that's that.

NORMAN. Aye, it's a crying shame, this drought, but Lord knows George'd be better set to tackle the old lady were he able first to tap the steward.

GEORGE *finally finds his voice.*

GEORGE. Trouble is I hardly ever touch whisky. The fact is, I don't really enjoy it.

NORMAN *and* DOCTOR MACLAREN *are flabbergasted.*

DOCTOR MACLAREN. Well, if you'll permit a medical opinion, George, that's half your trouble. If you'd fortified yourself as regularly as we have you'd not be giving tuppence about telling your mother you're to be married.

GEORGE (*eagerly*). I'll get it...

Belatedly, CONNIE *or* FLORA *ring a doorbell. They've been waiting for* BEA*'s arrival into the scene. At the same time* ANNAG NO. 1 (BEA) *passes through on a bicycle. If the space won't allow for an entire bicycle, the bell and handlebars* (*and possibly basket*) *might do.* ANNAG *crashes into the wings then returns to approach the door.* ANNAG*'s glamorous look may be influenced by Lana Turner in* Slightly Dangerous. *Her blonde wig and costume need to be highly distinctive, as four of the Pallas Players will portray her across the evening.*

CATRIONA (*looking towards* ANNAG). Ach, who can that be at this hour?

GEORGE *answers the door.*

ANNAG. Sorry to bother you, George. Is Doctor Maclaren here at all? He needs to come to Snorvig straight away.

GEORGE. It's young Annag MacRurie, doctor.

CATRIONA. It sounds urgent, doctor. You get off now – we'll see you again later in the week?

DOCTOR MACLAREN. Absolutely, Catriona. Compliments to the finest chef in these two islands.

CATRIONA. Oh, now, Doctor Maclaren...

DOCTOR MACLAREN *collects his bag and heads off, but then turns back into the room.*

DOCTOR MACLAREN. It seems unlikely I'll be able to drive you back to Garryboo, George – so I'm afraid you'll be on shank's mare. (*Creeping up behind* GEORGE.) It is my hope you'll make it home in time to share your splendid news with mother...

DOCTOR MACLAREN *invests that final line with comic menace, rolling the 'r' in 'mother' in a sneak preview of what we might witness when we meet the woman herself – who is also, of course, played by* WIN. GEORGE *looks petrified.* DOCTOR MACLAREN *exits to* ANNAG.

ANNAG. Ah, at last, doctor, there you are.

DOCTOR MACLAREN. What is it, Annag? You seem flustered.

ANNAG. I've bicycled all the way from Snorvig. It's old Alec MacPhee. I stopped to wish him goodnight as we passed on the street, and the next thing I knew he'd collapsed at my feet.

DOCTOR MACLAREN. Have you had men collapse at your feet before, Annag?

ANNAG. Never the ones I like, Doctor Maclaren.

DOCTOR MACLAREN. Such is life.

ANNAG. Aye. Anyway, I managed to get him indoors, which was no mean feat, doctor, for though Captain MacPhee's a great age, he's a big strong man, not unlike yourself.

DOCTOR MACLAREN. You were right to fetch me, Annag. I'll drive there directly.

ANNAG (*taking his arm*). I'll cadge a lift, doctor.

DOCTOR MACLAREN. What about your bicycle, Annag?

ANNAG. It's not my bicycle.

MONTY *steps forward…*

MONTY. Meanwhile, in the Snorvig Hotel bar, Annag's father, Roderick, had spent another evening gloomily surveying a gaggle of dispirited men – who in turn had spent another evening eyeing with increasing mournfulness their pathetic glasses of beer; for to a serious drinker – we may have some amongst us – beer's not worth the candle lest it be chasing a dram.

The Bar at the Snorvig Hotel

RODERICK MACRURIE (DORIS) *presides over* DROOBY
(AILEEN) *and* NORMAN (JULIET). THE BIFFER *is out in
the gents – he'll arrive once* FLORA *is ready.*

RODERICK. You're saying George is set to tell his mother
tonight, Norman?

NORMAN. That was his plan, aye. All things being equal he
and my sister'll be married this summer.

DROOBY. All things are seldom equal when George's mother
is involved. I wish him the best of luck telling Mistress
Campbell.

RODERICK. For sure Catriona'll make George a good wife.
There's no better cook in Todaidh Mòr[4] than your sister.

DROOBY. Still, I can't imagine George having the courage to
tell Mistress Campbell such news. He'd need to have drunk
a dram the size of Loch Sleeport itself.

RODERICK (*aggravated*). And where might he get such a
dram in the midst of this drought?

THE BIFFER (FLORA) *enters, adjusting his trousers.*

THE BIFFER. I believe Drooby was speaking hypothetically,
Roderick. But he's right: on Mistress Campbell's part,
George can only expect obdurate intransigence.

DROOBY. Gents, aye – and what's more who'd blame George
for being hypathetic in the face of Mistress Campbell?

DOCTOR MACLAREN (WIN) *enters.*

NORMAN. Ah, Doctor Maclaren – how's the patient?

DOCTOR MACLAREN. Did old MacPhee seem all right when
he left here, Roderick?

RODERICK. He'd had his two pints, doctor, then he asked for a
third. I told him: 'I'm sorry, Captain, the way things are with

4. *Todaidh Mòr* [todday more] – Great Todday.

the shortages no man can have more, and, unless it comes by Monday's boat, the beer will be where the whisky is, and that's nowhere at all.' And didn't MacPhee turn on his heels then, lads, and without a word walk out of that door?

THE BIFFER. That's a fair simulacrum.

DROOBY. Crumb, aye.

DOCTOR MACLAREN. Well, as you know, young Annag fetched me to MacPhee after he'd collapsed in the street. He's gone, I'm afraid. (*Pause.*) D'you know, to my sure knowledge, Alec MacPhee has downed three whiskies and three beers every night for the past fifteen years.

NORMAN. What's your implication, Doc?

DOCTOR MACLAREN. MacPhee's had not a dram for twelve days, and now tonight he was denied his third pint. Let me assert with clear-eyed confidence that what caused the death of Old MacPhee was a critical lack of whisky and beer.

NORMAN. It makes sense.

RODERICK. We're all miserable worms in the eyes of the Lord. He might stamp us out with ne'er a second thought.

DROOBY. To think MacPhee stood right where you are now, Norman, not an hour since.

NORMAN *shifts slightly.*

THE BIFFER. In his ninetieth year, hale and hearty and seemingly set to outstay us all.

DOCTOR MACLAREN. Well then. (*Defeated, he heads off.*) I suppose some of you will go along to the house to sit with the body?

THE BIFFER. Aye, don't you worry yourself for that, doctor.

DROOBY. We'll be along there now and see to the wake.

THE BIFFER *and* DROOBY *now also head on out.*

RODERICK. It's a lot to take in, so it is. The Captain went terrible quick.

NORMAN. Perhaps it's better that way. It can never end well for any of us, so it's a blessing if our exit be brief.

RODERICK. Such are the ages of man: we are born; we get married; we die.

As MONTY *steps forward,* WIN *should be well on her way to becoming* MRS CAMPBELL.

MONTY. By the time George Campbell had completed the nine-mile hike from the schoolhouse at Watasett to the schoolhouse at Garryboo, it was very late – but contrary to his hopes and expectations, and despite a dogged lack of urgency, his mother was still not abed. Mrs Campbell at seventy-five was a majestic woman with an icy stare, given to energetic displays of contempt.

The Schoolhouse at Garryboo

GEORGE (AILEEN) *and* MRS CAMPBELL (WIN).

MRS CAMPBELL. What a time to appear, George! Where on earth have you been?

GEORGE. I was due to get a lift back with Doctor Maclaren, but he was called away to attend to Captain MacPhee, who'd collapsed in the street – so I'd to walk.

MRS CAMPBELL. I'm not at all surprised to hear about MacPhee. I'm told he took to reading his Bible last year, but what good it could do a man so steeped in drink I couldn't say. You haven't been up at the bar tonight yourself, have you, George?

GEORGE. No, Mother. What makes you ask that?

MRS CAMPBELL. You've been in the vicinity of Doctor Maclaren, and that man is never far from a bottle or jar.

GEORGE. You couldn't be more wrong. There's not a drop of whisky on the island. There's a shortage on account of the war.

MRS CAMPBELL. The Lord is merciful indeed. Well, if you've not been drinking, what have you been doing all this time, George? Where did you have your tea?

GEORGE. I um… went along to see Norman Macleod at Watasett.

MRS CAMPBELL. That good-for-nothing radical. Fine company you keep. I don't know what the Education Authority is thinking, letting a rascal like that corrupt the minds of children.

GEORGE. Norman's going into the Air Force.

MRS CAMPBELL. That's no surprise. He's not had both feet on the ground since he started walking. His mother, of course, spoilt all her children disgracefully. Not least that sister of his.

GEORGE. It was Catriona who kindly cooked us such a splendid meal.

MRS CAMPBELL. A rattleplate of a girl, just like her mother.

GEORGE. In point of fact, Catriona looks after her brother exceedingly well.

MRS CAMPBELL. You'd do well not to 'point of fact' me, George. What do you know about being looked after? You've had nobody but your mother to look after you since the day you were born. You'd soon learn the difference were you foolish enough to marry one of these modern girls. Well, George? What have you to say for yourself?

GEORGE. Nothing, Mother. I think I'll off to bed.

Snorvig House

WAGGETT (BEA) *dictates*. DOLLY (JULIET) *types*. DOLLY *wears her housecoat and her hair is awry*.

WAGGETT. 'To Major P St John Quiblick, Security Intelligence Corps, No. 14 Protected Area. Dear Major Quiblick, it is my duty to let you know that there appears at present to be a wave of defeatism in these islands. It has, I am afraid to say, affected the Home Guard to some extent and I think it might be worth your while to... investigate the phenomenon. I remain entirely at your disposal. With kind regards, Yours sincerely, Paul Waggett, Capt HG.'

DOLLY. I do hope you're not overreacting, Paul.

WAGGETT. One's responsibilities are not always clear-cut, old lady. The trained military mind must always recognise the call to action.

DOLLY. Of course, dear: what with the pen, as it were, being mightier than the sword.

WAGGETT. Not sure I follow your logic, Dolly. (*Reaching for his binoculars.*) Who's that heading this way?

DOLLY *sees* FRED (CONNIE) *approaching.*

DOLLY (*rushing off*). Why it's Fred Odd.

WAGGETT. Finally the Sergeant Major deigns to pay us a visit. I hope you feel suitably privileged, old girl. Just so long as he doesn't expect us to roll out the red carpet and dance a Hooley Hooley in his honour. (*Realising she has gone.*) Dolly?

A bell rings as FRED *arrives.* DOLLY *appears, hair immaculate, housecoat jettisoned, lipstick applied.*

DOLLY. Why, Sergeant Major Odd. What a lovely surprise.

FRED. 'Fred', Dolly, please. I hope we know each other well enough not to stand on ceremony.

DOLLY. Well, it's sweet of you to say that... Fred, but Mr Waggett, as you'll know, likes things just so. Oh, but I'm sure that lucky girl of yours has been overjoyed to have you back.

FRED. 'Lucky', Dolly?

DOLLY. Lovely's what I meant. It's turning out to be such a year for romance. I heard a rumour that George Campbell and Catriona Macleod are engaged. Can you imagine how Mrs Campbell will react to such a match?

FRED. Between you and me, Dolly, I'm having rather a torrid time myself: pinning Joseph down to a date when I might marry Peg.

WAGGETT *suddenly looms.*

WAGGETT. Ah, I thought I heard voices. Shall we go into my den, Sergeant Major? No doubt Mrs Waggett has household chores to be getting on with.

DOLLY *exits.*

Are you well? I myself have just managed to outmanoeuvre an extremely threatening cold.

As WAGGETT *and* FRED *move into the den, they are joined by* PADDY NO. 1 (AILEEN), *an overgrown Irish setter, who, overjoyed to see* FRED, *leaps up excitedly, greeting him like a long-lost friend.* FRED *attempts to calm* PADDY *down.*

FRED. I don't think I was ever in this room before.

WAGGETT. No, I only really made up my mind to have a den last year, when Mrs Waggett invited her sister to stay for what turned out to be the entire summer.

FRED. One's in-laws, I imagine, can prove stressful.

WAGGETT. Yes, it's a sort of bolthole, I suppose. A chap needs a patch to call his own.

FRED (*losing his battle with* PADDY). I say, sir, any chance you might…?

WAGGETT. What's that? Oh. Paddy! Get down! Find Mummy, there's a good boy. (*Shouting off.*) Dolly!? Dog!

DOLLY (*off*). Here, Paddy. Paddywhack!

PADDY *is off and away.*

FRED. Your authority remains wholly undiminished, sir. So how are things with G Company? No doubt they're smart as guardsmen by now.

WAGGETT. If only that were the case, Sergeant Major. I'm afraid Home Guard attendance has been falling for some time, but lately we've reached rock bottom. There were just two at the last parade; two that is, until one of them decided his time was best spent elsewhere.

FRED. Oh, dear. So who was the poor fellow left parading on his lonesome?

WAGGETT. That'd be me, Sergeant Major.

FRED. Ah. Well, sir, in mitigation, I think folk hereabouts are feeling a touch of war-weariness as a result of these shortages. From what I can make out they've not been without whisky for thousands of years. It's like depriving them of the very air they breathe.

WAGGETT. Nonsense. They drink far too much whisky when it is available; a shortage ought to be character-forming. The thing is, once the initial danger of immediate German invasion faded, all their keenness drained away. I'm very fond of Todday folk, but they do lack staying power. Hopefully, Sergeant Major, you'll get time to drum up that old keenness and make them take their training seriously again.

FRED. I shall do my best to buck things up, sir. Now, Major Wyndham-Pitts has summoned me to Glenbogle day after tomorrow, following which I'm up at Cloy with Sir Hubert Bottley; but why don't you drop Colonel Wolseley a line, see if he can't sort something out?

WAGGETT. You're awfully popular, Sergeant Major. I shall insist we need your services just as soon as you can be spared. In the meanwhile, I wonder if it wouldn't be a good idea to run you round the island tomorrow in the Austin. Just so the locals can register you're back amongst us, as it were.

FRED. As you like, sir. But I shall have to pop over to Kiltod at lunchtime, as I've arranged to drop in on Father Macalister.

WAGGETT. Not a problem, Sergeant Major. I can come with. I try to see as wide a range of natives as possible on a relatively regular basis. I do believe they find my presence here somewhat... reassuring.

MONTY *steps forward...*

MONTY. The next day, as promised, Sergeant Odd hopped into Mr Waggett's Austin for a spin. First stop: the schoolhouse at Garryboo. Had our hero been making the trip by less mechanical means, he might have enjoyed observing the bountiful birdlife of this island paradise. Regard the lapwing flouncing overhead, peewitting noisily away...

Who's Perce?

Hark! To hear the crying of the whimbrel...

Who's Perce?

And might that be a corncrake grating in the ditch?

Who's Perce?

On Board Waggett's Austin Sixteen

WAGGETT (BEA) *drives erratically.* FRED (CONNIE) *holds on tight.*

FRED. Terrible news about old MacPhee, sir. I was sorry not to get the chance to see him one last time. He'd some wonderful yarns about the old windjammer days.

WAGGETT. Of course you'd to take a good deal of what he said with a hefty pinch of salt. I got up a Brains Trust in the church hall, and we got on to Jonah and the whale. I pointed out that anybody with the most elementary knowledge of natural history knew that a whale couldn't swallow anything larger than a sardine, but MacPhee was adamant I was talking nonsense.

FRED. Watch out, sir…

*A couple of black-face sheep have wandered into the road,
causing* WAGGETT *to break suddenly and honk his horn.*

WAGGETT. Confounded things. (*Drives on.*) Where was I?

FRED. Call me Ishmael.

WAGGETT. Ah, yes. So I said, 'You're not going to tell me that
you were ever eaten by a whale, Captain MacPhee?' And
while he admitted he'd personally never been consumed, he
would insist he'd met a man who had. The audience actually
clapped. So I quipped, 'Well, Captain, the whale may have
swallowed your friend whole, but I'm wholly unable to
swallow your tale.' And, d'you know, the audience didn't get
my joke. Simply sat there like a lot of dummies.

FRED. Wasn't that the schoolhouse we just passed?

WAGGETT. Ah, yes. (*Slams on the brakes then goes into
reverse.*) Here we are.

FRED. Thank goodness.

The Schoolhouse at Garryboo

As WAGGETT *and* FRED *arrive,* MRS CAMPBELL (WIN)
emerges.

WAGGETT. Ah, Mrs Campbell, good day. You'll remember
Sergeant Major Odd. He's back from Africa, so we're to
have the benefit of his advice once again.

MRS CAMPBELL. Advice about what?

WAGGETT. Training the Home Guard.

MRS CAMPBELL. Ah. Fred Karno's army. You were better
occupied, perhaps, in Africa.

FRED. Actually, Mrs Campbell, we rather hoped we might have
a word with George, regarding the old 'ragtime infantry'.

MRS CAMPBELL. My son is teaching school, Sergeant Odd, and cannot be disturbed. At Watasett perhaps they do things differently, but at Garryboo we consider education sacrosanct – pupils are supervised at all times.

WAGGETT. Who knows, Mrs Campbell, perhaps one day there will be little Odds amongst their number. You may be aware that Sergeant Major Odd plans to marry Peggy Macroon?

MRS CAMPBELL. I'm surprised to hear that, Sergeant. A man of your age. Are you a Roman Catholic?

FRED. No, Mrs Campbell, I'm not.

MRS CAMPBELL. Yet you're proposing to marry a Roman Catholic?

WAGGETT. Well, perhaps if George is unavailable, Sergeant Major, we ought to be getting along. We have quite enough to do this morning.

FRED. It's a queer thing, Mrs Campbell: earlier Captain Waggett was lamenting the falling off in shooting practice as regards the Home Guard. But there doesn't seem much wrong with Cupid's aim in these parts. He's a proper marksman on both of the Toddays, by all accounts.

MRS CAMPBELL. I have not the slightest idea to what you are alluding, Sergeant Odd.

FRED. Forgive me, Mrs Campbell. Didn't I hear earlier on the grapevine that we've also good reason to congratulate your son?

MRS CAMPBELL. Congratulate my son on what?

FRED. Why on his forthcoming marriage to Catriona Macleod. A lovely girl it must be said; and the finest cook on these two islands, by all accounts. You must be very proud.

MRS CAMPBELL. George. George! GEORGE!

GEORGE (AILEEN) *rapidly appears.*

FRED. Ah, there you are, Mr Campbell. Look here, old chap, any message for your intended? We'll be calling at Watasett shortly to catch up with Sergeant Macleod.

GEORGE. 'Intended'? (*Notices his mother's expression.*) Ah. I see. No... no message.

FRED. It's been a pleasure, Mrs Campbell.

FRED *and* WAGGETT *exit.*

MRS CAMPBELL. I'm waiting, George, for an explanation.

GEORGE. I planned to tell you the other night, but couldn't get a word in edgewise.

MRS CAMPBELL. The bed I have made for myself and on which I must lie. This comes of spoiling my only child.

GEORGE. Of spoiling me?

MRS CAMPBELL. Now in my old age I must reap as I have sown. To think that I would hear from others that my own son is to be married!

GEORGE. I was wary of upsetting you. After all, I could be certain you wouldn't approve.

MRS CAMPBELL. So you knew it would upset me, and you were sure I would not approve, yet you decided to press ahead regardless with this sham proposal.

GEORGE. It's not a sham proposal. I mean to marry Catriona. She's a very nice girl.

MRS CAMPBELL. Perhaps you'll allow your mother to know better than you about nice girls. Miss Macleod's filching family have always been amongst the idlest and most disreputable of the Great Todday crofters. It's common knowledge that even now a great deal of what graces the table of that schoolhouse at Watasett is poached from under Mr Waggett's foolish nose by that good-for-nothing socialist Norman Macleod.

GEORGE. We must move with the times, Mother. A lot of well-respected people are socialists nowadays.

MRS CAMPBELL. There'll be no 'moving with times' when your eternal soul is in torment.

GEORGE. I don't understand this resistance, Mother. After all, apart from disapproving of her brother's politics, you've no logical reason to dislike Catriona herself.

MRS CAMPBELL. I cannot be expected to give my approval to the sort of girls who go gallivanting over to Obaig for lipstick and permanent waves.

GEORGE. I'm sure if you took the trouble to get to know Catriona you'd understand my feelings. So, when I bring her to tea on Saturday I hope you'll be nice to her, Mother.

MRS CAMPBELL. I'll warn you now, son: if that Macleod girl ever sets so much as a lacquered toe inside this house I will be away to live with my sister in Kircudbright.

GEORGE. You despise the mainland! And you've not spoken to your sister for sixty-five years.

MRS CAMPBELL. Blood is thicker than water, George!

GEORGE. I am your blood! And Catriona Macleod is the girl I love!

MRS CAMPBELL. I see you're hell-bent on breaking to pieces this poor old woman's heart. (*Starts to walk off.*) I cannot bear it, George. I'll hear no more!

GEORGE. Mother! (*Addressing the heavens.*) Give me strength.

MONTY *steps forward…*

MONTY. Back on board the Austin, Sergeant Odd devised a strategy of putting his thoughts elsewhere while Waggett prattled on. As the car drove southward he was comforted by the familiar sound of a curlew fluting far away…

Who's Perce?

…and gazing longingly across the Coolish to Little Todday, it occurred to him with some annoyance that he seemed to have spent more time with Captain Waggett lately than in the tender arms of his betrothed.

On Board Waggett's Austin Sixteen

As WAGGETT *drives erratically,* FRED *has his head out of the window.*

WAGGETT. You're very quiet, Sergeant Major.

FRED. Sorry, sir – miles away.

WAGGETT. She's very bigoted of course: Mrs Campbell, I mean.

FRED. One does feel for George, in thrall to that fossilised old pterodactyl. She's a regular pantomime villain, that's for sure.

WAGGETT. Couldn't say, Sergeant Major – not one for the theatre – more at home with a novel. Have you read *The Garrotted Announcer* by Peregrine Potter? It begins with the discovery of the body of a BBC announcer, a Mr Humphrys, then proceeds backwards to the incident that incited the crime, while at the same time / moving forwards through the ensuing investigation…

MONTY *steps forward…*

MONTY. Serendipitously for Alfred Odd – and indeed for us – the Captain had grossly mistimed his egregious assault on the tiny canon of Peregrine Potter: as our duo had now arrived at the schoolhouse at Watasett.

The Schoolhouse at Watasett

As WAGGETT *and* FRED *arrive,* NORMAN (JULIET) *comes out to meet them.*

NORMAN. I thought I heard the Austin, Captain Waggett; but here's a pleasant surprise: Sergeant Major – always good to have you back.

FRED. I appreciate that, Mr Macleod.

They shake hands.

NORMAN. No doubt you'll be wanting to discuss the soon-to-be vacant position of section commander for Watasett, Captain Waggett, what with me away to the Air Force.

FRED. Ah, yes, you're off into the blue. No doubt the Germans'll be wondering what's hit them.

NORMAN. That's right, Sergeant Major, I'm looking forward to having / a crack at Jerry...

WAGGETT. Before we get on to that, Sergeant Macleod, there are more pressing matters to address.

NORMAN. Crikey. Sounds ominous...

WAGGETT. There's no easy way to say this, Sergeant Macleod: I'm concerned about the growing slackness of the Home Guard. Something has to be done to remind the men they're under military discipline. I'm afraid I'm seriously considering the advisability of prosecuting one or two of the worst shirkers.

NORMAN. That won't achieve anything, Captain. Prosecutions simply put people's backs up.

WAGGETT. You misunderstand, Sergeant – I don't want to prosecute; I take no pleasure in it. I could've prosecuted certain people for poaching, but never have. Unfortunately, the command of the Home Guard isn't my private affair. We're at war – and we must all to do our bit in the fight to preserve England. I mean Britain.

NORMAN. If Jerry's capable of invading, I don't see how we might prevent it.

WAGGETT. Such statements, Sergeant, smack of rank defeatism. I'm surprised by your attitude, Macleod; it comes as a painful shock to hear one of my own men hover so perilously close to collusion.

NORMAN. I take great exception to that slanderous remark, Mr Waggett. Were this a peacetime conversation, I'd presently be taking off my jacket.

WAGGETT. Ah, now we're seeing the firebrand of legend. D'you hear this, Sergeant Major? Idle threats and bellicose behaviour. How easily the natives resort to type.

NORMAN. Why you insufferable, stuck-up sassenach twit, I've a good mind to...

They square up to each other. NORMAN *would happily skelp* WAGGETT; *while* WAGGETT*'s aggression is mere bravado.* CATRIONA (DORIS) *rushes on to help separate them.*

CATRIONA. What on earth's this commotion?

NORMAN. I'm being grievously insulted within earshot of my own pupils, Catriona.

FRED. Calm down, the both of you. I'm sure Captain Waggett wasn't meaning to cast aspersions, Mr Macleod. Nobody knows better than he what a lot of hard work you've put in with the Home Guard. Sir?

WAGGETT. Look here. Sorry if I hurt your feelings, Mr Macleod. I'm simply anxious Odd shouldn't take up his duties again only to find there's nobody to command and nothing to be done.

NORMAN. The Sergeant Major's always been well-liked, Captain; if he can convince G Company they're not wasting their time, no doubt he'll be supported.

CATRIONA. How utterly ridiculous you both looked, facing off like a couple of stags.

FRED. Actually, Miss Macleod, I rather think I have an apology of my own to make. To you, as it happens.

CATRIONA. I can't think why, Sergeant.

FRED. Thing is, I may have inadvertently broken the news to Mrs Campbell about your engagement to her son.

CATRIONA *hugs him, delightedly. He's rather taken aback.*

CATRIONA. God bless you, Fred Odd. (*Exits*.)

> MONTY *steps forward.* FLORA *is almost prepared to be*
> FATHER MACALISTER, *but she retains one last vestige of*
> MONTY (*his hat*) *before she makes complete the change.*

MONTY. Our duo's next port of call was to Father Macalister,
the portly priest of Todaidh Beag...[5] (*Removes her hat and
adopts her* FATHER MACALISTER *accent.*) who was very
much looking forward to entertaining a full half of their
number. In the meanwhile he passed a happy hour rereading
Destry Rides Again.

The Chapel House at Kiltod

The bell sounds. FATHER MACALISTER *looks up from his
book, then comes to greet* FRED. WAGGETT *hovers.*

FATHER MACALISTER. Great sticks alive, Sergeant, by
Jiminy I'm glad to see you. How are you, my boy?

FRED. Oh, I'm in the pink, Father.

FATHER MACALISTER. Good shooting.

FRED. And how are you?

FATHER MACALISTER. Holding on, Sergeant, despite the
rotten state of Denmark. Here's an old friend returned from
barbarous places like Africa and Devonshire, yet I'm unable
to offer him even the most minute sensation.

WAGGETT. 'Sensation', Father Macalister?

FATHER MACALISTER. Uisge beatha,[6] man – a dram!

WAGGETT. Oh I never drink before lunch, as it happens.

FATHER MACALISTER (*contemptuously*). Ach, it's not you
I'm worrying about, Colonel, it's Sergeant Odd.

WAGGETT. Quite. Well, if you'll excuse me, Sergeant Major,
perhaps I'll take this opportunity to collar Joseph Macroon

---

5. *Todaidh Beag* [todday beck] – Little Todday.
6. *Uisge beatha* [ooshki beh-ha/oosh-ka bay-ah] – Water of life (whisky).

about proper observance of the blackout. Thank you for your hostility, Father. (*Leaves*.)

Once WAGGETT *is out of earshot,* MACALISTER *aims an imaginary six-shooter in the direction of his departing, and quotes from* Destry Rides Again...

FATHER MACALISTER. 'No one but a fool would present a broad target, such as a back, to Destry.' (*Fires, then blows smoke from the barrel of his imaginary gun, before reholstering.*) You must forgive me, Sergeant, I can't abide that chucklehead. And Joseph'll not listen to a blind word either; he'll cock a deaf ear while the fool pontificates.

FRED. Yes, I've observed that behaviour from Joseph myself, of late. Each time I try to pin him down to a date for the wedding, he switches subject to something else. In the end I held out for Easter week, and he held out for not discussing it till summer's over. I don't suppose you've any advice, Father?

FATHER MACALISTER. My advice is to roll right over Joseph and marry Peg at Easter. She's a lovely girl. Roll right over him, I say.

FRED. But he's very difficult to roll over, Father. He's slippery as an eel.

FATHER MACALISTER. I'll speak to him, my boy. I'll tell him he's to have the wedding at Easter. And if he won't agree, by Jove, I'll roll over him myself.

FRED. I'm awfully grateful, Father. You've been jolly decent to me right from the start.

FATHER MACALISTER. You're a straight-shooter, Sergeant – the kind I like.

FRED. Look here, Father, as regards Peg and me. I'd always imagined that all our children would be brought up Catholic same as their mother. Well, I've been thinking things over and... er... I didn't want to say anything before I was sure you were in favour of our marriage but... um... the upshot is, having given it a good deal of consideration, I believe I'd rather like to become a Catholic myself. So, Father, there you have it.

FATHER MACALISTER. Aye, and a mighty big 'it' it is, Sergeant. You'll require instruction.

FRED. I'll do whatever it takes, Father. I want to make it right, for Peggy's sake.

FATHER MACALISTER. I can see you do. I'll write to Father MacIntyre at Drumsticket and ask him to supply the needful.

FRED. I'm afraid he'll find me pretty ignorant.

FATHER MACALISTER. Never you mind, Sergeant. The less you know the easier it'll be.

FRED. One other thing, Father. I wonder if this could be kept quiet for now? I wouldn't like the old man to think I was trying to get round him.

FATHER MACALISTER. As you like it, Sergeant. We'll not say a word.

FRED. Then once it's fixed up I'll tell Peggy first.

The bell of the chapel house sounds again.

FATHER MACALISTER. Doggone my eyes, this'll be just the fellow we need.

As DUNCAN (JULIET) *enters,* FLORA *momentarily reverts to being* MONTY, *by donning* MONTY*'s hat.*

MONTY. Duncan Macroon – the bard of Todaidh Beag!

FLORA *removes the hat to become* FATHER MACALISTER *again.*

DUNCAN. Yes, I'm your man, Father Mac. Hullo, Sergeant – I'm glad to find you here.

FATHER MACALISTER. We're to have a wedding the week after Easter, Duncan. You're to start composing a ballad for the happy couple telling what a magnificent fellow the Sergeant is and what a perfect match he'll make for his marvellous bride…

DUNCAN. Peg is a fine girl too, Sergeant. But how am I to compose such a beauty of a tribute with no liquid inspiration? No fiddler can fiddle his best without a bit of resin for his bow.

FATHER MACALISTER. It won't stay this way forever, Duncan. *The Island Queen* will be in on Tuesday.

DUNCAN. Suppose the boat comes but the whisky never does, Father? It's not possible to plan any sort of ceremony with just tea and ginger ale. Even if there was plenty beer a whiskyless wedding would be a crime against nature.

FATHER MACALISTER. Have faith, my son – and see if both inspiration and libation don't arrive in good time. All we have to do, Duncan, is go right ahead and spread the word about the Wednesday after Easter – that's April 28th – and by all the holy crows, you'll see – the Sergeant and Peggy will be married on that date! Darn tootin'!

FRED *can be straight into the next scene.*

The Harbour at Kiltod

PEGGY (AILEEN) *and* FRED *are snatching a moment before* FRED *goes back to the mainland.*

FRED. It's going to be all right, Peggy darling. Father Macalister is going to tackle your dad. He and Duncan Macroon are going to tell everybody it's all fixed up for April 28th. Oh, Peggy, I can't believe I have to be away again already. It's as if I've hardly seen you. How we'll enjoy each other once we're together for always.

PEGGY. You're very sure of yourself, Fred.

FRED. I'm just blissfully content – thanks to Father Macalister understanding everything so well. 'Peg o' My Heart', eh? (*Sings.*) 'Come be my own, come make your home in my heart...'

PEGGY. Oh, Fred.

FRED. Sorry. I know I'm not much of a crooner.

PEGGY. It's not that.

FRED. Then what?

PEGGY. If only you weren't a Protestant.

FRED. Well, I am, and there it is.

PEGGY. Yes, there it is, I suppose.

> MONTY *steps forward, as* AILEEN *becomes*
> LIEUTENANT BOGGUST *– disguised as* MR BROWN.

MONTY. When *The Island Queen* arrived on the Saturday, she still carried no whisky, but now there was not even a barrel of beer on board, meaning Roderick MacRurie was forced to cut the allowance to half a pint a day. Disembarking that trip was a queer fish indeed. A young man sporting plus-fours of the barrage-balloon variety. Despite his unconventional attire, nobody paid much attention to the stranger on the pier that afternoon, and so, carrying his own luggage, he perambulated up to the hotel to bag a room.

The Reception at the Snorvig Hotel

ANNAG NO. 2 (WIN), *is on reception, reading her movie magazine.* MR BROWN (AILEEN) *enters. He's English. A bell is rung – though there seems to be no need. On entering any new space* MR BROWN *has developed a tendency to perform a sort of forward lunge or split squat, the better perhaps to proudly display his voluminous trousers in all their glory.*

ANNAG. Yes?

MR BROWN. I'd like to book a room.

ANNAG. We have rooms.

MR BROWN. As I anticipated. I'd like to secure one for two nights.

ANNAG. A secure one?

MR BROWN. To secure one.

ANNAG. You require two rooms?

MR BROWN. I require one room. For two nights.

ANNAG. Are these rooms required for you?

MR BROWN. This room. One room. Yes... of course.

ANNAG. And you are?

MR BROWN (*as if rehearsed*). I am travelling in tweed. My brief is simply to enquire into the manufacture and / availability of local...

ANNAG (*impatiently*). Name?

MR BROWN. Ah. Of course. Brown. William Antony Brown.

ANNAG. Would you be spelling that with an 'h', Mr Brown?

MR BROWN. Would I be spelling what with an 'h'?

ANNAG. I'm thinking 'Anthony' can be spelled with an 'h'.

MR BROWN. Don't be ridiculous.

ANNAG. As in Anthony Quinn. Or indeed your Anthony Eden.

MR BROWN. In this instance it's A-N-T-O-N-Y, as in... *Antony and Cleopatra*.

ANNAG. And will Cleopatra be joining you, Mr Brown?

MR BROWN. Just give me a room, young lady...

ANNAG (*handing him a key*). Room two. Down the corridor.

MR BROWN *marches off.* MONTY *steps forward.*

MONTY. Mr Brown spent the evening in the hotel bar listening in on the conversations of various local characters, making notes, and occasionally proffering his own wholly unsolicited opinions on various political and military matters. Later still, under cover of darkness, he was observed heading off in the direction of Snorvig House.

Snorvig House

A bell rings. DOLLY (JULIET) *wearing her dressing gown –
and perhaps a face-pack – greets* MR BROWN.

MR BROWN. Brown. Tweed merchant. To see Captain Waggett.

DOLLY. Is my husband expecting you?

MR BROWN. That is my belief, ma'am.

DOLLY. Paul! There's a funny little man at the door. Paul!
    PAUL!

  WAGGETT (BEA) *appears, also dressed for bed, carrying*
  The Garrotted Announcer *by Peregrine Potter.*

MR BROWN. Brown, sir.

DOLLY (*exiting*). He says he's a tweed merchant.

WAGGETT. I really can't think who would recommend you
    call on me, Mr Brown. I've absolutely no pertinent
    information to convey in relation to the tweed trade.

MR BROWN. You've not had word from Major Quiblick, sir?

WAGGETT. Let's adjourn to my den. I'm sure there's a sensible
    explanation. I was just rereading Peregrine Potter's *The
    Garrotted Announcer*. Do you know it?

  As WAGGETT *and* MR BROWN *enter the den* PADDY
  NO. 2 (DORIS) *launches himself at* MR BROWN, *perhaps
  pinning him in place.* WAGGETT *won't notice, as he has his
  back turned and is going through a pile of mail.*

MR BROWN. I'm afraid not. Hello there, boy. Good dog. Nice
    dog. Big dog. Ow.

WAGGETT. It's a Crime Club thriller, providing a fascinating
    glimpse into what goes on at the BBC. Ah… what's this?
    'Very Secret'. From Major Quiblick. I'd not got to it yet, old
    chap. (*Reads.*) 'Dear Captain Waggett…'

  MAJOR QUIBLICK (CONNIE) *appears to continue the
  letter. He speaks frighteningly posh English.*

QUIBLICK. '…much obliged for your letter of the 22nd inst. Lieut. WA Boggust arrives Snorvig Saturday 27th inst. to investigate the matter to which you referred. He will travel under the name of WA Brown, his apparent object being to enquire into the tweed industry on both islands. I have instructed him to contact you upon arrival. You may rely absolutely on his discretion. Sincerely, P. St John Quiblick, Major…'

QUIBLICK *disappears*. WAGGETT *will shortly turn back to see* MR BROWN *and* PADDY *entwined*.

WAGGETT. '…Security Intelligence Corps.' So it all becomes clear. Ah, you've met Paddy. Get down, boy! Paddy! Get down! Find Mummy, there's a good boy. (*Shouting off.*) Dolly!? Dog!

DOLLY (*off*). Here, Paddy. Paddywhack!

PADDY *is off and away*.

WAGGETT. You have a very interesting job, Mr Boggust.

MR BROWN. I'd rather you called me Brown, sir – if that's alright. I believe it best to preserve one's cover at all times.

WAGGETT. Quite safe in here, old boy.

MR BROWN. But I'm tremendously thorough. I try to think of myself as Brown, d'you see? I've been sat in the hotel bar this evening merging seamlessly with the locals. (*Gets his notebook out.*) I'd not been in situ five minutes before a fellow called 'The Biffer' could be overheard detailing the whereabouts of a son serving in the Mercantile Marine. Loose lips sink ships, Captain Waggett. Later, I'm sorry to report, the BBC came in for criticism.

WAGGETT. I'm not surprised. They'd sooner suffer the atmospherics from Athlone than enjoy the finest reception from the Home Service. I've even had reports that some of them listen regularly to the German wireless.

MR BROWN. Extraordinary! Don't they realise there's a war on? Personally I'd make it a penal offence to listen to the enemy. We can learn a lot from the Germans, in that regard.

WAGGETT. Quite, if there's one thing you can say for the Germans, it's that they're very thorough.

MR BROWN. Absolutely. Anyway, a bit later, I'd just started explaining to the locals how we export whisky to America in order to help pay for our war expenditure, when a chap with a high-pitched voice piped up: (*Impersonating* WIN *as* DONALD.) 'If we're winning the war, like your BBC says, why don't the government give us our own whisky? Cos when these Americans have finished drinking every drop we'll like as not find it'll be they've won the war and not ourselves at all.'

WAGGETT. You'll find the islanders prize highly neither logic or consistency. What I find annoying is that people who'll believe a lot of nonsense about the Loch Ness Monster give no credence to the idea that Hitler might invade us. I sometimes wonder if such people don't actually deserve to be under enemy occupation. (*Yawning*.) But look here, it's Sunday shortly. If it were Monday you could go round the island looking for lengths of tweed, but you can't do that on Sunday.

MR BROWN. What about Little Todday? That's a Catholic island, isn't it? They'd not pay any attention to Sunday there, I suppose?

WAGGETT. You couldn't get across. People here won't use their boats on Sunday; you'll be pretty much confined to barracks, I'm afraid.

BOGGUST. Well, I'd better be getting back to the hotel. Sorry for waking the house, Captain Waggett, but fetching up earlier risked blowing my cover.

WAGGETT. No matter, Mr Brown. Mum's the word.

MR BROWN *is pushed out into the night. Checking he isn't watched, he skulks off.*

MONTY *steps forward.* WIN *is supposed to be at the Dansette putting on a recording of rain falling. She's slightly late.*

MONTY. When Mr Brown looked out of the windows of the hotel after breakfast on Sunday morning, it was pouring with rain, causing him to feel that rampant defeatism, if unjustifiable, was at least understandable.

The Lounge of the Snorvig Hotel

The sound of rain. MR BROWN *stares miserably out at the weather.*

MR BROWN. Service!

ANNAG NO. 3 (CONNIE) *appears alarmingly swiftly.*

ANNAG. What can get you, Mr Brown?

MR BROWN. Ah... Annag. I'd like some whisky please.

ANNAG. I'm afraid you're after having all the whisky you can be having, Mr Brown.

MR BROWN. But I haven't had any.

ANNAG. There's a shortage.

MR BROWN. Then how about you bring me half a pint of ale?

ANNAG. You had your half-pint earlier. The way things are we can't be serving anybody more than half a pint of beer a day. Will that be all, Mr Brown?

MR BROWN. Given that you can offer me nothing of what I require, Miss MacRurie, one might very well conclude that the service at the Snorvig Hotel is consistently superfluous.

ANNAG. You're very kind, Mr Brown. (*As she leaves.*) I'll pass that on to father.

WIN *removes the needle from the rain record.*

MR BROWN. An extraordinarily primitive people. (*Looking out of the window.*) And still it rains.

WIN *rushes forward and puts the record back on, but* FLORA *sighingly signals for her to take it off. In doing so,* WIN *scratches it.*

MONTY *steps forward. During his speech,* FLORA *becomes* THE BIFFER.

MONTY. Mr Brown's visit to the Toddays was not a success. He was received everywhere with sheepish stares, suspected of being a snooper from various government ministries – real and imagined. One house confidently proclaimed him a German spy, solely on the grounds that even an Englishman wouldn't be caught sporting such ridiculous britches. But by the following Saturday the locals had pretty much forgotten all about Mr Brown – until, on that frore foggy whiskyless night, a motley crew converged in Roderick's joyless bar.

The Bar at the Snorvig Hotel

RODERICK (DORIS) *waves an envelope at* DONALD (WIN). DROOBY (AILEEN) *and* THE BIFFER (FLORA) *arrive as soon as can be managed.*

RODERICK. I've been blessed with official correspondence, Donald. On His Majesty's Service.

DONALD. Why is the King writing to you, Roderick? Would it be about the whisky shortage?

RODERICK. It's from a Major Quibalick at the Security Intelligence Corps at Nobost Lodge. Would you listen to the cheek of him? (*Reads.*) 'Sir, I have received a most unfavourable report…'

As RODERICK *starts to read* QUIBLICK (CONNIE) *appears and takes over.*

QUIBLICK. '…regarding the bar at the Snorvig Hotel. I understand conversation in your establishment at times constitutes careless talk and is often critical of the conduct of those who carry upon their shoulders a great weight of military responsibility. Nothing could encourage Hitler more than a belief that the British people lack confidence in their leaders. I trust you will remind your patrons that careless talk costs lives, and take immediate steps to improve the general atmosphere thus avoiding the unpleasant necessity…'

QUIBLICK *disappears.*

RODERICK. '…of further action.' Atmosphere? There was never a finer atmosphere in the whole of the Islands. Didn't the Duke of Ross himself congratulate me on the air in this hotel? 'It is better than that in my own castle, Mr MacRurie', is that not what he said?

THE BIFFER. I can't claim to have been present, Roderick, but I recollect you contemplated having those very words inscribed on a plaque and exhibited for posterity.

DROOBY. Austerity, aye.

RODERICK. So who's been snooping about and submitting reports to this Quibalick?

THE BIFFER. You need look no further than that fellow Brown who was staying in the hotel. I took him over to Kiltod.

DONALD. I thought I recognised the squit. He's no Brown. He's Boggust. Lieutenant Boggust. Didn't I bring him to Nobost about a month ago, and didn't he come up on the bridge and nearly drive me daft with his questions.

RODERICK. The tweed merchant, is this?

DROOBY. Tweed merchant! All the tweed he ever bought he put round his own arse.

As she says this, AILEEN *may not be able to resist a forward lunge, in the manner of* MR BROWN.

THE BIFFER. Let the rascal come back here, I'll kick the wee dobber off the end of the pier.

WAGGETT (BEA) *enters. The atmosphere declines.*

WAGGETT. Evening, everybody. The fog's extremely thick, I'd the devil of a job finding my way to your door, Roderick. Nearly fetched up at the church hall.

RODERICK. You'd have found as much to drink there as you'll find here, Mr Wackett.

WAGGETT. Sorry to hear supplies are still short. But we must remember each drop of whisky we don't drink does help pay for the war.

DROOBY. As does every drop we do, the way it's taxed. And I'd sooner pay for the war by drinking whisky, Mr Wackett, than by not drinking it at all.

WAGGETT. That's not the reason I'm here. I'm afraid I've received a letter from Major Quiblick of the Security Intelligence Corps.

RODERICK. Och, I've had a letter myself from this Quibalick, Mr Wackett. Some people have nothing better to do than write letters.

WAGGETT. Well, if Major Quiblick has written directly to you, Roderick, I shall say no more.

THE BIFFER. Donald has just been illuminating us all, as regards your Mr Brown.

WAGGETT. Brown, you say? Doesn't ring any bells.

DROOBY. That's somewhat surprising, as he was seen visiting your house.

WAGGETT. Ah, you refer to the tweed merchant?

DONALD. He was no tweed merchant.

RODERICK. He's one of your pocket Hitlers from Nobost.

WAGGETT. Well, what a turn-up. He certainly fooled me.

THE BIFFER *exits towards the gents*.

THE BIFFER. Then indubitably he must be a master of disguise.

WAGGETT. Anyway, I'd best not stop. Dolly will be frantic. Oh, before I go – Captain MacKechnie, d'you think you'll get away in time to be back in Snorvig on Tuesday? I only ask because I'm expecting Sergeant Major Odd.

DONALD. I wouldn't care to give to an answer about that in weather like this, Mr Wackett. We were lucky to make the island at all – the fog came round us so quick.

WAGGETT. Understood. Well, as you were. (*Exits*.)

MONTY steps forward. CONNIE at the Dansette for sirens and cows.

MONTY. It was the following day, a Sunday, that the people going into church at Snorvig heard the siren of a ship sounding to the north-west…

Sound of siren.

…just as the people coming out of church at Kiltod heard it sounding away to the north. Some time later, in thick fog, Joseph Macroon caught up with Duncan Macroon at the head of Macroon's Bay.

Macroon's Bay, Little Todday

DUNCAN (JULIET) *attempts to stare out across the bay.* JOSEPH (DORIS) *catches up, puffed out. It's so foggy they can see almost nothing.*

JOSEPH. Duncan. I thought I recognised your kingfisher-blue scarf through the gloom.

DUNCAN. And I caught a glimpse of your red knitted hat, Joseph Macroon.

JOSEPH. What did you make of that siren?

DUNCAN. It came from the north.

Distant sound of a cow.

JOSEPH. Is that her again now?

DUNCAN. That's a heefer. A lovely, melancholy sound…

JOSEPH (*unconvinced*). It could give a man the wullies.

DUNCAN. This fog's so deep I can barely see in front of my eyes.

JOSEPH. Ach, it's probably cleared out there. She'll have run into better weather.

DUNCAN. Listen.

A 'Hallo?' can be heard through the fog.

JOSEPH. Did you hear that? (*Afeared*.) That's no creature I can name.

A 'Hulloo?' can be heard through the fog.

DUNCAN. I believe there's more than one.

Assorted hallos and hulloos can be heard through the fog.

DUNCAN. Hush. They're getting closer.

JOSEPH. They're almost upon us, man....

ROBBIE BAIRD (BEA), *a red-haired Clydeside man, pops up behind them. He carries a map.*

ROBBIE. Hulloo.

JOSEPH (*almost jumping into* DUNCAN*'s arms*.) Whit the heck?!

ROBBIE. Could you tell us where we are, pals?

JOSEPH *extricates himself gingerly.*

JOSEPH. You're right here, man, all of a sudden.

DUNCAN. You're on Little Todday, friend.

ROBBIE. Our cutter's made fast to the rocks, halfway up the bay. The fog lifted for a bit after we struck, so the master volunteered muggins here to accompany him ashore.

CAPTAIN HEADLEY-FAVERSHAM (CONNIE) *appears, and extends his hand to the islanders, introducing himself in his West Country accent.*

HEADLEY-FAVERSHAM. Headley-Faversham. Nice of you boys to set up a welcoming committee.

JOSEPH. Joseph Macroon.

DUNCAN. Duncan Macroon.

HEADLEY-FAVERSHAM. Father and son, I presume?

DUNCAN. Distant relatives.

JOSEPH. At best. You can think yourself lucky to have come in where you did, Captain. You might easily have had yourselves lost.

DUNCAN. The fog's clearing, Joseph. I can almost see her.

A cut-out of the precariously-placed Cabinet Minister *becomes visible somewhere on the set.*

JOSEPH. She's a huge great ship.

ROBBIE. *The Cabinet Minister.* Four thousand tons. Blue Limpet Line. Bound for New York.

DUNCAN. She's lying terribly crooked.

HEADLEY-FAVERSHAM. Looks worse than it is. She may float off at high water.

JOSEPH. I'm pretty sure she'll not.

ROBBIE. Och well, if she's a job for salvage, at least she's safe from Fritz.

JOSEPH. You'd better not be staying aboard any longer than you have to.

HEADLEY-FAVERSHAM. Most of the crew are already off and in the boats.

DUNCAN. You're in luck, the mailboat got into Snorvig yesterday and couldn't leave again.

JOSEPH. That's not to say she'll take you back to Obaig tonight.

DUNCAN. They're very strict about the Sabbath on Great Todday.

JOSEPH. They're Protestants – we're all Catholics here.

DUNCAN. No matter, you'll do well enough at the hotel. Though there's very little beer.

JOSEPH. And no whisky at all.

HEADLEY-FAVERSHAM. No whisky, eh?

JOSEPH. There's not been as much whisky as you'd get in a poorhouse for two months now.

HEADLEY-FAVERSHAM (*to* ROBBIE). That sounds bad, chief, don't it?

ROBBIE *and* HEADLEY-FAVERSHAM *produce hip flasks and hand them to* JOSEPH *and* DUNCAN.

JOSEPH (*drinks*). Am I dreaming, or is this Stag's Breath?

ROBBIE. You're a connoisseur, Mr Macroon.

HEADLEY-FAVERSHAM (*to* DUNCAN). And that, my friend, is known as Bard's Bounty.

DUNCAN. It is not so much you're dreaming, Joseph, but that we've died and gone to heaven.

ROBBIE. Drink deeply, lads, there's plenty more. We've fifty thousand cases on board.

JOSEPH. Are you pulling my leg, son?

HEADLEY-FAVERSHAM. Fifty thousand cases of whisky. That's our cargo, gentlemen.

DUNCAN *and* JOSEPH *turn to each other as* ROBBIE *and* HEADLEY-FAVERSHAM *consult their map.*

JOSEPH. Fifty thousand cases of whisky?

DUNCAN. And twelve bottles in every case?

JOSEPH. Glory be to God and to His Blessed Mother and to All the Holy Saints.

DUNCAN. Didn't Father Macalister tell me we just had to have faith?

HEADLEY-FAVERSHAM. So let's get this clear, chaps. Little Todday's where we are. Great Todday's where we need to be.

JOSEPH. Snorvig, aye.

HEADLEY-FAVERSHAM. And you're quite certain there's no chance of her floating off on the next tide?

JOSEPH. Not a hope, Captain.

DUNCAN. Cannae see it happening.

ROBBIE. Then we'll row the lifeboats round to Snorvig, sir?

HEADLEY-FAVERSHAM. I'm wondering if it might be sensible to leave a couple of lads on board till the salvage crew arrive.

JOSEPH. Och, it's calm enough just now – and for sure none of us would care to tempt fate – but if there's anything of a swell she couldn't be in a worse place...

DUNCAN. Joseph's right. Heaven forfend if the weather turns again – it'd prevent any poor soul from getting ashore...

JOSEPH. Och, but you'll know best...

HEADLEY-FAVERSHAM. No. No doubt you're right. The old lady may be a lame duck, but let's have no loss of life. For your help we're much obliged.

DUNCAN. We'll send word to Snorvig from Kiltod that you'll be there before sunset.

HEADLEY-FAVERSHAM. Appreciated. Now then, as it's been so long since you've had a drop, perhaps you'd each take one of these to tide you over. Goodbye, gentlemen.

ROBBIE *and* HEADLEY-FAVERSHAM *produce two bottles of whisky, hand them to* DUNCAN *and* JOSEPH, *then exit.*

ROBBIE. So long, lads.

DUNCAN. Is that not the most beautiful sight, Joseph?

JOSEPH. And there's six hundred thousand bottles still on board. Uisge beatha gu leòir![7]

They are so moved that they find themselves inadvertently hugging. Then, arms still entwined, bottles gripped in their free hands, they turn out to face the audience.

DUNCAN *and* JOSEPH. Whisky galore!

On the Dansette, perhaps Jim Cameron & his Scottish Dance Band playing 'The Fiddler's Joy'.

End of Act One.

---

7. *Uisge beatha gu leòir* [ooshki beh-ha gul-yor] – Whisky galore.

ACT TWO

CONNIE *at the Dansette – perhaps a brief taste of Jim Cameron & his Scottish Dance Band playing 'Corn Rigs'.*

The Pier at Snorvig

Sunday night. Cut-out boats loaded with cases of whisky can be seen leaving the cut-out Cabinet Minister.

THE BIFFER (FLORA)*, restless, checks his pocket watch.* DROOBY (AILEEN) *arrives.*

THE BIFFER. Drooby, man. Where have you been?

DROOBY. I was up at the hotel having a crack with the crew of *The Cabinet Minister.* They're all going aboard *The Island Queen* now.

THE BIFFER. She's away tonight?

DROOBY. Within the hour, the Captain said. I've been thinking – say we were just to take a boat and edge round the north side of Todaidh Beag to have a look – no one could call that breaking the Sabbath.

THE BIFFER. I suggested as much to the missus, Drooby, but she was adamant to the contrary: 'Let the ship bide till Monday,' she reiterated, ad infinitum.

DROOBY. Item, aye. But is a wife's advice always in a man's best interest? D'you think on Little Todday they'll let the ship bide till Monday?

THE BIFFER. The very point I countered with, my friend. You seem intent on mirroring our domestic altercations with scrupulous exactitude.

DROOBY. Chewed, aye. But I'm not sure it'd be breaking the
Sabbath just to have a wee keek.[8]

THE BIFFER. Well, it's your prerogative to interpret the
theology as you see fit. But I'm anxious neither to defy the
wife nor incur the wrath of God. I'll take the *Kittiwake* out
on the stroke of twelve to see what's what. It'd be a pity to
let them over yonder have all that whisky.

DROOBY. They'll never get it all, Biffer. There's thousands of
bottles in *The Cabinet Minister*. You couldn't drink it all, not
if you lived forever.

Midnight strikes.

The Cabinet Minister

A golden decrescent moon illuminates JOSEPH (DORIS) *and*
DUNCAN (JULIET) *as they unload whisky from* The Cabinet
Minister *into* The Morning Star. DUNCAN – *perhaps up a
ladder – lowers cases down to* JOSEPH.

DUNCAN. It's an epic ballad, Joseph, falling into my lap
almost fully formed: Bonnie Doon, Highland Heart, Prince's
Choice, Mountain Tarn… Fiona's Farewell, Salmon's Leap,
Lammermoor… They'll be poets rare and true, Joseph, to
dream up names like these.

JOSEPH. Will we get it ashore, Duncan – and save the recital
for another time? It's past midnight.

THE BIFFER. Ahoy there!

JOSEPH. Here's company…

DUNCAN. It's Drooby and The Biffer. Ahoy, lads! You've
reached Rainbow's End.

DROOBY *and* THE BIFFER *come alongside in the*
Kittiwake.

JOSEPH. You've been a long time coming.

8. A wee keek [a wee keek] – A little look.

DROOBY. We'd to wait till the Sabbath was over.

DUNCAN. No matter, there's enough for everybody from the Butt of Lewis to Barra Head. Here's a start for you, lads.

DUNCAN *gives them the case he's just brought down.*

JOSEPH. You'd best take a dram to prepare for your labours.

JOSEPH *breaks open one of his bottles and passes it to* DROOBY. *It passes between the four of them throughout what follows, ending up with* DUNCAN *just before he and* JOSEPH *leave.*

DROOBY. Slàinte mhór.[9] (*Drinks.*) A Chruithear,[10] that's beautiful stuff.

JOSEPH. Don't spare it, a bhalaich.[11] There's more bottles of whisky on board than the biggest catch of herring you've ever had.

DROOBY. What is it?

JOSEPH. Annie Laurie.

DUNCAN (*sings*). 'For bonnie Annie Laurie I'd lay me down and die…'

THE BIFFER. A tiny taste of heaven permeated with sublime iridescence.

DROOBY. Sense, aye – I'm sensing this might be the greatest night of our lives.

DUNCAN. 'Sweet Moon, I thank thee for thy sunny beams…'

THE BIFFER. 'I thank thee, Moon, for shining now so bright.'

JOSEPH. Aye, aye! One thing to bear in mind, lads. The Bard's Bounty is to go to Duncan here. Apart from that, it's all up for grabs.

DUNCAN. When were they saying in Snorvig that we'd see the salvage men?

9. *Slàinte mhór* [slahnje vor] – Great health.
10. *A Chruitheir* [a crooyer] – O Creator.
11. *a bhalaich* [a vahlich] – O boy.

THE BIFFER. Perhaps with Tuesday's boat.

JOSEPH. We'll endeavour to make their job as easy for them as we can.

DUNCAN. We've a rope ladder rigged up going down into the hold.

JOSEPH. We've shifted quite a load. I've been backward and forward a dozen times or more.

DUNCAN. But you won't see the difference, there's that many cases on board.

JOSEPH. So long as the weather keeps good we'll all get a tidy few out of her.

DUNCAN. Take another dram afore you start, lads. You've a hard night ahead.

The bottle is passed to DROOBY *as* DUNCAN *and* JOSEPH *head off in* The Morning Star. DROOBY *drinks, passes it to* THE BIFFER, *then investigates the case.*

DROOBY. Annie Laurie, eh, Biffer – I hope we hit on a case of that.

THE BIFFER. Time is of the essence, Drooby, for we're late to the party. There's the weather to think about, and the salvage, and no doubt the Excise'll be along – not to mention the polis. You need to be on your mettle, man – for you'll be up and down like the Giessbach Funicular.

DROOBY. Cooler, aye. But I'm thinking a dram might be wise, to help keep the cold air off our chests. (*Brandishes two bottles.*) What's your choice? Lion Rampant or Tartan Perfection?

THE BIFFER. We'll try Lion Rampant. But just a nip, mind.

THE BIFFER *opens the bottle.*

DROOBY. Aye, but if we don't then try Tartan Perfection who's to say which has the edge?

DROOBY *opens the other bottle. They drink from one, then the other, on through the scene.*

THE BIFFER. Ach, I don't know which is best.

DROOBY. I'll take another draw of Lion Rampant just to test.

THE BIFFER. It's becoming no clearer.

DROOBY. I can't decide either.

THE BIFFER. Will we try Tartan Perfection again? It's a pity not to know which is the superior.

DROOBY. I've concluded it's impossible to choose between them, but I do feel distinctly content.

THE BIFFER. I'll not deny, Drooby, I note a marked improvement in my own demeanour. Slàinte mhath![12]

DROOBY. Slàinte mhór! Well, old pal, though some say they're close in Little Todday, I'd not say that at all.

THE BIFFER. I wouldn't say it myself. Slàinte mhór to all our friends on Little Todday.

DROOBY. Slàinte mhór! Did they begrudge us even a bottle?

THE BIFFER. They never did. 'Help yourselves, boys,' that was the spirit.

DROOBY. I swear so long as there's whisky in the country, I'll never see a Little Todday man go without a dram.

THE BIFFER. Never!

DROOBY. Never!

They fall asleep.

12. *Slàinte mhath* [slahnje vah] – Good health.

Snorvig House

WAGGETT (BEA) *dictates*. DOLLY (JULIET) *types. She's in
her housecoat and her hair is dishevelled.*

WAGGETT. 'To Major P St John Quiblick, Security Intelligence
  Corps. You will have been informed by now of the wreck of
  The Cabinet Minister, but may not be aware that the islanders
  are 'recovering' as much as they can of the cargo of fifty
  thousand cases of whisky. I am unable to put the Home Guard
  in charge of the situation without official authorisation.
  I needn't point out how much the danger of careless talk will
  be increased by a flood of 'free-for-all' whisky let loose in the
  vicinity. Yours sincerely, Paul Waggett.'

  DOLLY *thinks they've finished the admin for the day.*

  One more, old girl. 'To Mr Thomas Ferguson, Exciseman.
  I regret to inform you that *The Cabinet Minister* remains
  without guard. Hundreds of bottles of whisky on which no
  duty has been paid are already in circulation. As a taxpayer
  I resent seeing potential revenue being poured down the drain.
  Yours truly. Paul Waggett, OC Home Guard.' (*Sighs.*) One can
  only hope, Dolly, this will have some effect. I really do feel
  both islands are now on the verge of complete moral collapse.

DOLLY. I wonder, Paul, if people won't think you're interfering
  in things that might better be left to take their course.

WAGGETT. The breakdown of civilised behaviour, Dolly, is a
  serious matter.

DOLLY. That's all very well, dear, but when in Rome…

  WAGGETT *sees* FRED (CONNIE) *approaching.*

WAGGETT. Ah, here's Sergeant Major Odd, headed up the
  path. Thank heaven for another highly trained military mind.
  Much as I love living here, Dolly, I do feel we suffer from a
  deficiency of operational perspicacity. Dolly?

  She has gone, for just as soon as the bell rings, isn't DOLLY
  *there opening the door with perfect hair and make-up, but,
  alas, with her housecoat still on.*

FRED. Dolly! It's as if you wait behind the door anticipating my approach. For every time you spring out fresh and lovely as a daisy.

DOLLY. Oh, gracious. I must apologise, Fred. I'm still in my housecoat.

FRED. And never did a housecoat seem so eminently chic.

DOLLY. Gosh, what fabulous nonsense you speak.

WAGGETT looms, pushing DOLLY aside.

WAGGETT. Ah, thought I heard voices. I'll take over from here, Dolly. Come through to the den, Sergeant Major, I'm anxious to catch up. How was the shooting yesterday at Garryboo?

As they step into the den, PADDY NO. 3 (WIN) *appears, overjoyed to see* FRED.

FRED. Encouraging, sir. Sergeant Campbell was in particularly good form.

WAGGETT. The Home Guard is making a new man of George Campbell. We seem to have given him a boost in self-confidence.

FRED. Credit too, the love of a good woman, sir. Though I suspect it'll take a miracle to persuade his dinosaur of a mother to give that union her blessing.

WAGGETT. Paddy! Get down! Find Mummy, there's a good boy. (*Shouting off.*) Dolly!? Dog!

DOLLY (*off*). Here, Paddy. Paddywhack!

PADDY is off and away. FRED *wipes slobber from his tunic.*

WAGGETT. I understand you're soon to tie the knot yourself, Sergeant Major?

FRED. We're banking on late April – but Peggy's pa's proving hard to pin down.

WAGGETT. It's impossible to pin Joseph Macroon down to anything. (*Beat.*) All this is proving a heavy responsibility for me, Sergeant Major.

FRED. For you, sir?

WAGGETT. I feel I ought to put the Home Guard on *The Cabinet Minister* until the salvage crew arrive. But despite all my efforts to make G Company a crack unit, I ask myself, Sergeant – can I trust my own men? That's a fearful thing for an officer to have to face after nearly three years in command.

FRED. Might I speak plainly, sir?

WAGGETT. By all means.

FRED. With respect, sir, your opposition to the Home Guard helping themselves from the wreck has hit company morale. It'd be better, sir, if you turned a blind eye. The men know that in all likelihood that whisky's going to be dumped overboard; so as they see it they're preventing an abominable waste.

WAGGETT. I can't accept that view, Sergeant Major. The islanders have no right to suppose they know better than the authorities. Consider Roderick at the hotel. Will he welcome your future father-in-law flooding the market with *Cabinet Minister* contraband? I'm surprised to find you defending such a deplorable lack of discipline.

FRED. I'm not saying that the people are right, sir. I'm simply trying to understand their point of view.

WAGGETT. And by doing so you condone the continuance of a state of affairs which as good as constitutes complete anarchy! (*Beat.*) Sorry, Sergeant Major. I'm just very disappointed: with the men; with the powers that be; and – though I oughtn't say it – with myself. Used to getting things done, d'you see.

FRED. Yes... I... um... I ought to be going, sir. Said I'd meet Peggy and Duncan. We're visiting chums asking them to keep April the 28th free. I don't suppose you and Dolly... Mrs Waggett... would care to join us on that date, should we get a fair wind and a following sea?

WAGGETT. I couldn't possibly commit, Sergeant Major. It's my understanding that Mrs Waggett hasn't a stitch to wear when it comes to social functions. But we do of course appreciate the thought.

MONTY *steps forward.*

MONTY. Tom Ferguson, the exciseman, failed to acknowledge receipt of Captain Waggett's letter; while Major Quiblick wrote back to say that under no circumstances must the Home Guard meddle in matters not of their concern. The salvage company arrived and worked steadily at emptying the wreck, but they couldn't watch the ship around the clock. For a fortnight the cargo went into the sea by day and over the sea by night. Then, after a series of gales, *The Cabinet Minister* broke in half...

The model/cut-out of The Cabinet Minister *breaks in half. One half sinks.*

Outside the Post Office, Kiltod

JOSEPH (DORIS) *has been attending to his store of whisky when* DUNCAN (JULIET) *arrives.*

JOSEPH. Ah, Duncan, just the man. I've been having another wee stocktake. This one's rightfully yours.

JOSEPH *hands* DUNCAN *a bottle of Bard's Bounty.*

DUNCAN. Hello, my beauty. (*Kisses the bottle.*) I've enough inspiration for a thousand ballads, Joseph, yet still each night I struggle to get this wedding tribute right.

JOSEPH. You're jumping the gun, Duncan, as regards my daughter and the Sergeant Major; I've given no permission for any ceremony.

DUNCAN. You're not a man, surely, Joseph, to stand in true love's way.

JOSEPH. I've more important matters to consider, Duncan, than love, true or otherwise. Whisky, man. The shed's stocked to bursting, but is it secure? I've been thinking maybe to inter the entire stash away at the burial grounds yonder. There's plenty of ancient forebears planted there could keep it safe from raiders.

DUNCAN. Aye, there's plenty eejits, too – digging round for relics. You'd not want some tweedy archie-ologist to hie off with your haul.

JOSEPH. It'd take a brave person to tangle with the ghosts of the Macroons.

DUNCAN. Och, Joseph – why be afeared? What manner of thief is likely to furkle about on the premises of Kiltod's most prominent merchant?

JOSEPH. I have enemies, Duncan. Roderick MacRurie'll be on the warpath soon enough, mark my words. Apart from that, I'd not want the excise snooping about.

DUNCAN. Tell me, Joseph – how would you categorise your relationship with Tom Ferguson the exciseman?

JOSEPH. Tom knows which side his bread is buttered, I'd say.

DUNCAN. And Constable Macrae?

JOSEPH. Him and me have done some business over the past few days.

DUNCAN. Then it seems to me you're safe.

PEGGY (AILEEN) *has entered.*

JOSEPH. Hush now, Duncan. Ah… there's my daughter now…

DUNCAN. The Belle of Todaidh Beag.

JOSEPH. Abandoning her station to gallivant abroad with a host of feckless men.

PEGGY. I'd hardly call Duncan or Fred Odd feckless, father – or Great Todday 'abroad'.

DUNCAN. And I cannot speak for myself, Joseph, but Fred's a fine fellow – and a grand match for Peg. Now have you any message for your future son-in-law?

JOSEPH. Aye. Mind what I say and don't count your chickens. Now away and leave me be.

MONTY *steps forward...*

MONTY. While Joseph Macroon continued to cogitate and fret over where his not-inconsiderable amber bounty best be kept, our intrepid trio toured Great Todday in a borrowed car possessed of such disreputable character, such mechanical deficiency, and such tawdry appearance that we have elected to spare you sight of said conveyance; instead we shall make a small gap in time and skip straight to Garryboo. Here, Fred was to be foiled in his fancy that on this occasion he might engage with George – as opposed to the dragon...

The Schoolhouse at Garryboo

MRS CAMPBELL (WIN) *greets* PEGGY, DUNCAN *and* FRED (CONNIE).

MRS CAMPBELL. I'm surprised you've the brass neck to turn up here, Sergeant Odd, after the upset caused by your last appearance.

FRED. And good day to you too, Mrs Campbell. I'm sure it will come as no shock to hear I was actually hoping to see your son.

DUNCAN. You'll know Peggy Macroon, of course, Mrs C – the Sergeant Major's bride-to-be.

MRS CAMPBELL. Since you ask, Sergeant, George rushed off to Watasett an hour ago, no doubt on the whim of that flibbertigibbet Macleod girl.

PEGGY. Is it true, Mrs Campbell, that you've refused to allow Catriona across the threshold of your house?

MRS CAMPBELL. In my youth, Sergeant, young women had the good grace to keep silent on matters not of their concern. Nowadays it seems they'll chirp and chirrup about whatever takes their girlish urge.

DUNCAN *and* FRED *pipe up together…*

DUNCAN. Now hold your horses, missus…

FRED. I think you'll find, Mrs Campbell…

PEGGY. I can speak for myself, thank you, boys. We're all aware you place little value, Mrs Campbell, on opinions other than your own, but I'll tell you this: Catriona Macleod is one of the finest young women we know; and if your poor son has had the good fortune to somehow win her heart, then his bitter, twisted mother ought to thank her lucky stars.

A very brief pause while FRED *digests this hitherto unseen, tantalising version of his future wife.*

FRED. Gosh… So the thing was, Mrs C, we were hoping that we might persuade George to keep April the 28th free, as that's when we hope to have our celebration.

MRS CAMPBELL. Celebration of what?

DUNCAN. Their marriage, naturally.

MRS CAMPBELL. It doesn't seem 'natural' to me. Him being a Protestant and she… a Catholic. Furthermore, this so-called 'celebration' will, I imagine, provide yet more excuse for all concerned to souse themselves in this illegal liquor that's sloshing about. Suffice to say, Sergeant, George will not be attending.

DUNCAN. It's just a bit of a jollification, missus. It hardly / constitutes…

MRS CAMPBELL. Did the Lord send us into this world for jollification!? And as for you, Miss Macroon, what you rudely suggest is true: I'll not take tea with Miss Macleod, nor have her in my house indeed; and your unsolicited opinions cut no ice with me. My mind is set.

FRED. Well, we're sorry to hear that, Mrs Campbell, I'm sure. My own mind, on the other hand, remains open to change. In fact, I can tell you now that for the sake of my future wife's happiness, I'm currently in the process of becoming a Catholic.

PEGGY. Oh, Fred.

PEGGY *rushes to* FRED *and hugs him, then exits.*

DUNCAN. Aye, 'Oh, Fred', indeed. You might stick that in your pipe and smoke it, Mrs C.

MONTY *steps forward…*

MONTY. Peg returned to her duties at Kiltod pleased to have learned that her betrothed would be 'crossing the Tiber', as they say. The Sergeant and his bard, meanwhile, resolved to catch up with George Campbell at the schoolhouse at Watasett.

The Schoolhouse at Watasett

DUNCAN *and* FRED *approach the schoolhouse.*

DUNCAN. Wait a minute, Sergeant. (*Removing a bottle from his pocket.*) I almost forgot.

FRED. What's that?

DUNCAN. Courtesy of your future father-in-law. The Bard's Bounty. My inspiration, Sergeant, for your wedding ballad. Care for a sample?

FRED. After Mrs Campbell, I think I need it. Slàinte mhath.

DUNCAN. Slàinte mhór.

FRED. And yourself, Duncan, may I ask: how come you never married?

DUNCAN. Ach, the cailin[13] I wanted to marry met someone else. And so it goes.

FRED. Sorry, Duncan. It's just, when I think of Peg, I feel so darned happy. And I wish everybody else could feel that way.

DUNCAN. I've known 'lonely', Sergeant, truth to tell. But not for long. In the nick of time, Dionysus provides. (*Drinks.*) And now my days are golden.

13. *cailin* [callin] – maid.

CATRIONA (DORIS) *emerges in her Sunday best. She drinks from an enamel mug, into which at some point* DUNCAN *will absent-mindedly slip whisky.*

FRED. Hello. Somebody's off somewhere special by the look of it.

CATRIONA. Sergeant Odd. I presume you're here to take my so-called suitor into military custody?

FRED. On what charge, Miss Macleod?

CATRIONA. Cowardice in the face of a tyrannical mother.

FRED. Ah, well now. I'm sure he'll not be the first fellow ever accused of that.

DUNCAN. Although, in fairness to mothers everywhere, Mrs Campbell is an extreme case.

CATRIONA. I quite agree, Duncan. And extreme cases call for extreme measures.

FRED. Um. Where is George, actually?

CATRIONA. He and I have just had what I believe is called a frank exchange of views. I imagine he's indoors attempting to regather his forces.

FRED. Ah, I'd not like to get caught in any crossfire. I came to ask you both if you'd keep April the 28th free. That's the date Peggy and me are hoping to get wed. You'd both be very welcome to join the celebrations. It's not a copper-bottomed arrangement by any means, but Father Macalister assures me that if we just roll over her father, as it were…

CATRIONA. I'd love to come, Sergeant, thank you. And congratulations, you splendid man.

CATRIONA *hugs* FRED. *He's quite awkward about it.*

FRED. Oh, well now…

GEORGE (AILEEN) *emerges and is shocked to see his 'intended' in the arms of a soldier.*

GEORGE. What's going on? Ah. Sergeant Odd, it's you. Is Peggy not with you?

FRED. She was required on Kiltod, unfortunately.

CATRIONA. But we'll see her at the wedding party, obviously.

FRED. Well, yes… In fact we not long since called in at the Garryboo schoolhouse, Mr Campbell, specifically to invite you…

DUNCAN. But your mother informed us you'd be unable to attend.

CATRIONA. 'Unable', Duncan?

DUNCAN. 'George will not be attending', were Mrs Campbell's exact words, as I recall, Miss Macleod.

CATRIONA. Oh, George. After all we've said, this is still where we are. And did you even notice how I'm dressed, or wonder why…?

GEORGE. Well you look jolly nice, my dear. As you always do.

CATRIONA. I was intending to march, George, on Garryboo. I was going to demand your mother take tea with me. I'd been hoping that by now you might have found some pluck. No such luck. You're a wash-out, George, and what's more – it's your turn to wash up.

She thrusts her empty mug at him and exits, leaving him stood there rather pathetically, holding the mug to his chest. DUNCAN *pours some whisky into it.* GEORGE *drinks.*

GEORGE. So my mother attempted to prevent me, Duncan, from being present at your celebration, Sergeant.

FRED. That's right.

GEORGE *grabs the bottle from* DUNCAN *and takes a good slug.*

GEORGE. Well it just so happens… that on this occasion… indeed on all future occasions… and I'd ask you to witness this… (*Takes another good slug.*) yes… let me hereby declare… that my mother is… from this day forward… permanently and absolutely… (*Takes another good slug*.) undeniably, categorically, unequivocally, indubitably, and beyond any doubt… overruled! I will be at your wedding, Sergeant Odd, and what's more, I shall damn well be at mine! Catriona! Fetch your coat, hen! WE'RE TO TAKE TEA WITH MOTHER!!!

MONTY *steps forward…*

MONTY. Later that afternoon the balance of power seemed to shift in the Campbell household, thanks to a few home truths slurringly delivered by George, plus the mysterious power Catriona Macleod possessed to soften even the downright flintiest of hearts. Meanwhile, elsewhere on the islands – thanks to the continued surfeit of cheap whisky – tension and division had begun to grow and fester.

Snorvig House

WAGGETT (BEA) *looks through his binoculars and sees* RODERICK (DORIS) *approaching*.

WAGGETT. Dolly?! Dolly! There's someone at the door!

The bell rings.

I say, old thing – look lively!

DOLLY (*off*). I'm a bit tied up at the moment, bathing Paddy. Could you answer it yourself?

Perhaps brief noises off – splashing, whining, growling, gurgling – as DOLLY (JULIET) *gives Paddy his bath.* WAGGETT *reluctantly finds himself answering his own front door.*

WAGGETT. I've been half-expecting you, Roderick. Come through to the den.

RODERICK. I've left Annag holding the fort, Mr Wackett, but truth to tell it's like the *Mary Celeste* up at that hotel.

WAGGETT. I'm sorry to hear that, Roderick.

RODERICK. It's the whisky, Mr Wackett, is what it is. The way I see it, so long as Minnie's on these islands there's certain to be strife.

WAGGETT. Who's this 'Minnie' character, Roderick?

RODERICK. It's what they're calling the whisky they're securing from the wreck, Mr Wackett. *Cabinet Minister* – Minnie.

WAGGETT. How queer. Wouldn't 'Cabbie' have been more apt?

RODERICK. I don't know about that. I do know I've plenty whisky now, yet I've sold hardly a drop since this Minnie... Cabbie started going about. They fill themselves up with whisky at home then come to the bar for a beer to chase it down.

WAGGETT. I assure you, Roderick, I've done my best to get the authorities involved. I just can't seem to raise interest.

RODERICK. It wasn't so bad when they were just helping themselves to what they could drink, but now it's become a regular business. Joseph himself is selling it for three pounds a case. I cannot compete with that.

WAGGETT. It beggars belief.

RODERICK. There's only one solution, Mr Wackett. Ferguson the exciseman must come across and make an example of one or two. He'd be dropping in sharp enough, mind, were I to start selling Minnie myself.

WAGGETT. And what about Constable Macrae? I've found it nigh on impossible to get an audience with the man.

RODERICK. Ach, Macrae has a stash of Minnie down at the police station labelled 'confiscated' – but it can soon be liberated, you'll find – if the price is right.

WAGGETT. Most extraordinary.

RODERICK. Would you see your way to writing to this Major Quibalick, Mr Wackett? He seems an interfering kind of a chap. He wrote me a pretty fierce letter about the atmosphere at my hotel.

WAGGETT. You may rest assured, Mr MacRurie, that Major Quiblick will be hearing again from me. And we might both drop a line to the exciseman. Perhaps a pincer-type attack may prevail…

Nobost Lodge, Uist

QUIBLICK (CONNIE) *is just finishing a telephone call.*

QUIBLICK (*into telephone*). Yup. Yup. Roger that. See you anon.

He replaces the receiver, then sighs as he looks at the latest letter from WAGGETT.

BOGGUST (AILEEN) *enters. He's been unable to fully shake off his Mr Brown 'forward-lunge' mannerism. He may imagine he is about to be promoted for his 'undercover' work.*

BOGGUST. You wanted to see me, sir?

QUIBLICK. I've received yet more unwelcome correspondence from this Waggett chap. I'm starting to wonder if we don't actually need to be seen to be doing something. As you know, Boggust, apropos careless talk: I don't see barroom tittle-tattle as being a serious menace to security; but this sudden glut of whisky might spell havoc. Now, those Navy fellows can be pretty skittish, so I'm not anxious to interfere in anything that's not our pigeon.

Who's Perce? Perhaps JULIET *has been tricked into using the bird-whistle.*

Neither do I want to give the Home Guard an inflated idea of their own importance. But apparently they're selling this whisky now – at three pounds a case. Upshot is, I've asked Ferguson the excise chap to drop in for a jaw.

BOGGUST. Three pounds a case, sir? It must be frightful hooch.

QUIBLICK. First-class stuff, apparently. (*Beat.*) If any of us do get over to Snorvig, Boggust, we must be very careful.

BOGGUST. Absolutely, sir.

QUIBLICK. You do see what I'm saying?

BOGGUST (*he has no idea*). I'm not sure…

QUIBLICK. I'm wondering how many cases, Boggust, we might get hold of…?

BOGGUST. Ah.

QUIBLICK. Look here, this must be Ferguson, right on cue. We'll play it by ear.

FERGUSON (WIN) *enters. He's from Aberdeen. He swiftly identifies* QUIBLICK *and studiously ignores* BOGGUST, *who might hope in vain for at least a handshake.*

FERGUSON. Major Quiblick, I presume? Good afternoon.

QUIBLICK (*shakes hands*). Ferguson. Thanks for dropping in. I'm sure you're fearful busy. Thing is, we're a bit concerned about all this illicit whisky.

FERGUSON. I'll be frank with you, Major, I'm a bitty worried myself. At first I thought it wiser to leave things to the salvage, but since the ship cleaved asunder they've skedaddled till the fine weather. If the stuff's on sale, obviously I'm obliged to enquire into it; it may mean prosecutions, mark you.

QUIBLICK. A few prosecutions won't do any harm, surely?

FERGUSON. The last thing I need is to see old friends fined or sent to prison. Are you familiar with this Waggett?

QUIBLICK. He has made himself known to us. Right, Boggust?

BOGGUST. Yes, sir. I had the pleasure of meeting him / when I was visiting…

FERGUSON *seems to notice* BOGGUST *for the first time. He's not impressed. He addresses only* QUIBLICK.

FERGUSON. He's the interfering, bumptious sort, and I'm not eager to let him think he's cock o' the roost. But I've had a letter from big Roderick at The Snorvig Hotel so it's clear action must be took.

QUIBLICK. I propose we pay a surprise visit – avoid giving the locals advanced warning. We'll rendezvous with Constable Macrae and make a day of it.

BOGGUST. Maybe I'd be best employed here, sir – holding the fort, as it were, while you fight the philistines?

QUIBLICK. Very well, Boggust, I suppose you've earned a free pass. Boggust had a ticklish time on the Toddays, Mr Ferguson – he's not anxious to return. Might I suggest we start at the hotel? Mr MacRurie may be able to give us some pointers...

BOGGUST. You might want to interview young Annag while you're there, sir. Something of the Mata Hari about that one, to my way of thinking.

FERGUSON *turns to study* BOGGUST *momentarily, swiftly concluding that the lieutenant is as foolish as he appears.*

MONTY *steps forward...*

MONTY. A crisp clear day greeted Major Quiblick for his expedition to the Toddays. On the way from Snorvig pier up to the hotel his heart lifted at the simple natural splendour of the isles. He caught the cold disdainful eye of a squatting fulmar, as it chuntered and complained upon its rock.

Who's Perce?

And Hark! Was that not a lark ascending into the great wide blue?

Who's Perce?

Outside the Hotel at Snorvig

FERGUSON *and* QUIBLICK *in the shadows at the back of the hotel.*

FERGUSON. He said he'd meet us out back, Major Quiblick.

QUIBLICK. Why the cloak and dagger, Mr Ferguson?

FERGUSON. The islanders are never keen to be seen cosying up to the authorities.

QUIBLICK. But you gave me to understand it was MacRurie requested our presence.

RODERICK (DORIS) *steps out of the shadows, startling* QUIBLICK.

RODERICK. I'm glad you've come, Mr Ferguson. (*Shakes his hand.*) You'll find none of the stuff, of course, but the sight of you might serve as a warning.

QUIBLICK. So who are the chief culprits, Mr MacRurie?

RODERICK. Och, man, I'll name no names. They're all culprits if it comes to that. Are you from the excise yourself?

FERGUSON. No, no, Roderick. This is Major Quiblick, Head of the Security Intelligence Corps.

RODERICK. Quibalick! The man who wrote me a letter complaining of the atmosphere in my hotel. Quibalick, I'll not forget that name in a hurry.

QUIBLICK. It's Quiblick, actually.

RODERICK. I said Quibalick. Never was I having such a letter before. I'll have you know, Major Quibalick, that I took a great deal of offence at what you wrote.

QUIBLICK. I'm afraid there's a war on, Mr MacRurie. There's no time to worry about hurting folk's feelings; we're fighting for our existence as a nation, d'you see?

RODERICK. Which is why you sent your weaselly spy amongst us, I suppose.

QUIBLICK. Look here, MacRurie, if you're not prepared to cooperate, we'll interview your staff. Lieutenant Boggust raised the suspicion that this 'Annag' you employ might be some sort of exotic dancer working undercover for the enemy.

RODERICK. You've no business, Major Quibalick, mentioning my daughter in the same sentence as that knock-kneed nitwit Bogus Brown.

QUIBLICK. Ah, apparently Boggust failed to furnish me with the full facts.

RODERICK. There's a few fellows on the two Toddays anxious to furnish your Brown or Boggust with a fat lip, Major Quibalick, not to say a kick up the bracket. And if you want to speak to Annag, then you'll find her over at Kiltod, visiting her friend Peggy Macroon. Whether or not they'll be practising exotic dancing, I couldn't say, but I can guarantee you'll not find them insulting an honest man about the atmosphere in his own bar.

QUIBLICK. I can see we'll get no further here, Mr Ferguson, so I suggest we rendezvous with Constable Macrae and proceed to seek answers elsewhere.

RODERICK. Aye, it wouldn't be a bad thing if you had a word with Macrae. He takes it all too easy. I've plenty whisky now so it's aggravating to hear of non-licensed persons feathering their nests at my expense.

RODERICK *marches off.* MACRAE (FLORA) *emerges from the shadows. He's from Kintail, in the north-west Highlands.*

QUIBLICK. Not much help from that quarter, Mr Ferguson.

FERGUSON. Roderick's just anxious to cause a wee fright. He wouldn't want to get anyone into real trouble. Ah, here's Macrae now, Major. Constable…

QUIBLICK. Macrae. Quiblick. Glad you could make yourself available at such short notice.

MACRAE. Not sure why you need me, Major. I've enough to do without being responsible for ships. If the navy don't care and the salvage people aren't interested, I can't see what *The Cabinet Minister* and her contents have to do with the polis.

FERGUSON. The excise is taking an interest, as of now, hence my presence. And we'd be obliged if you'd just come across with us to Little Todday for a wee walk around.

MACRAE. But all the damage is done, Tom. The ship was wrecked a month ago, and here's the first we've seen of you. There'll be hundreds of cases hidden away by now all over the two islands. Whisky's so plentiful some of them are using it to wash their hands.

QUIBLICK (*aghast*). To wash their hands?

MACRAE. Och, soap's scarce and whisky takes the grease off fine. The women even use it for cleaning their windows and floors.

QUIBLICK. It's certainly high time we intervened. Now I wonder if it wouldn't be politic to ask Waggett to come along?

WAGGETT (BEA) *emerges from the shadows – ready to take part.*

FERGUSON. Captain Waggett? I don't think so, Major.

MACRAE. I'll second that, aye.

FERGUSON. What has Waggett to do with it at all?

MACRAE. I wouldn't want General Montgomery himself on a job like this, so we certainly won't require a man who merely thinks he's General Montgomery.

QUIBLICK. Oh, I don't press for him. This is no job for amateurs. Let's go to Kiltod.

QUIBLICK, FERGUSON *and* MACRAE *climb into their motorboat – the* Nellie.

Snorvig House/Outside Kiltod Post Office/The Harbour at Kiltod

WAGGETT *watches dejectedly through his binoculars as* QUIBLICK, FERGUSON *and* MACRAE *set off and, during what follows, cross the Coolish in the* Nellie. *He imagines that* DOLLY *is in the next room hanging on his every word. Meanwhile,* ANNAG NO. 4 (JULIET) *sits reading a magazine on Kiltod, while* PEGGY (AILEEN) *works the telephone switchboard.*

WAGGETT. Aha, Dolly. It seems Major Quiblick has persuaded the elusive Constable Macrae to emerge from his bunker. How extraordinary that it's entirely through my initiative that at last action is being taken, yet I appear, for some reason, to be persona non grata...

PEGGY (*on telephone*). Post office, Kiltod.

WAGGETT. It'll be jealousy, of course. It was the same in the last war. The professional soldiers couldn't bear me always being right.

PEGGY (*on telephone*). No, he's not. He's in Edinburgh all week.

WAGGETT. Remember how I told the Brigadier that the Germans would make their main thrust against us at Haut Camembert and not at Petits Fours? Suffice to say, if it hadn't been for my foresight we might very well have had a repetition of what happened in March 1918.

PEGGY (*on telephone*). Are you sure, now?

WAGGETT. Of course, I'm not comparing this whisky business to France and Flanders, but plus ça change, as the French would have it, plus c'est le même chose.

PEGGY (*on telephone*). And there's three of them?

WAGGETT. The point is, Dolly, had they deigned to include me on their little excursion I should have pointed out that by the time they reach Little Todday the smoke signals will already have arrived and every drop of illegal whisky be safely hidden out of sight.

WAGGETT *retreats, taking the binoculars with him.*

PEGGY (*on telephone*). Yes. Yes. I'm grateful to you. Goodbye, now. (*Removing her headset.*) Annag! We need to look lively, lass!

PEGGY *is looking for the binoculars.* BEA *has forgotten to put them back in the correct place.*[14]

ANNAG. What is it, Peggy?

PEGGY. Have you seen the binoculars? They've not been put back where they're supposed to be.

BEA *attempts an inconspicuous re-entry manoeuvre dangling the binoculars from her outstretched arm.* JULIET *isn't sure what to do.*

ANNAG. There they are…

PEGGY. Oh yes, hanging on that gnarled and rotten old tree. Pass them to me, would you?

ANNAG *takes the binoculars from the hideously embarrassed* BEA *and hands them to* PEGGY.

ANNAG. What is it, Peggy?

JULIET *and* BEA *share a look.* JULIET *is sympathetic.* BEA *exits awkwardly.* PEGGY *trains the binoculars on the harbour.*

PEGGY. The worst. (*Focuses the binoculars.*) Oh, dear. He's looking terribly fierce.

ANNAG. Who is?

PEGGY. The exciseman. He's with the Constable and a chap in a bowler hat. Once they reach the harbour, there's no doubt they'll be up here directly.

ANNAG. Why would they come here, Peg?

PEGGY. The shed's full of Minnie, of course – they'll have had a tip-off. Your father wouldn't have…

14. Perhaps mark this in earlier in the evening by having people almost forget to return the binoculars to the correct place.

ANNAG. Of course not, Peggy. He's no snitch.

PEGGY. I'm sorry, Annag, I didn't think it for a minute. What'll
we do? If they search the shed they'll put my father in
prison. We need to hide the whisky.

ANNAG. There's no time.

QUIBLICK, FERGUSON *and* MACRAE *disembark and
work their way back to the other side of the stage via the
audience. They are searching for whisky. They can use torches
to look into hidey-holes, under seats, in bags, etc. They will
search the harbour and then move up to the post office.*

PEGGY. Then there's only one thing we can do. We have to
make it disappear.

ANNAG. How's that now?

PEGGY. Well, I suppose we'll just have to… empty it away.
Annag, you try to keep your eye on where they've got to. I'll
get on and do the dreadful deed.

ANNAG. Peggy, I'm not sure…

PEGGY *starts to empty the whisky away as* ANNAG, *with
binoculars, comments on who owns the properties*
MACRAE, FERGUSON *and* QUIBLICK *are supposedly
searching.* DORIS *and* BEA *can also be pouring whisky
away, to add to the sound, if required.* PEGGY *shouts out the
names of the whisky brands as she pours them away.*

PEGGY. Where are they Annag?

ANNAG. Hold on. They've dropped by on Jockey
MacMulligan. He'll keep them talking, certainly. That
bletherskite could have the hind legs off a cuddie.

PEGGY. That's the Bannachmore and the Bonnie Doon doon
the drain…

ANNAG. They've extricated themselves and latched on to
Smiley O'Reilly. He was just closing up his workshop.

PEGGY. Farewell Fingal's Cave and bonnie Annie Laurie.

ANNAG. They have him unlocking it again. What a palaver. You'll find no grog in there, you eejits, he's teetotal. That's why he's crabbit. Even on a good day he's a face like a skelped arse.

PEGGY. Cheerio Albadhor and ta-ta Mountain Tarn...

ANNAG. They've moved on to Murdina McCartney at the bakery. She likes a man in uniform.

PEGGY. That's the last of Northern Light and the end of the Road to the Isles.

ANNAG. She's all over them like a clegg at a midden. They'll need to beat a swift retreat if they're to keep their reputations.

PEGGY. That's the last of the Highland Hope.

ANNAG. Ach, she's no shame that woman. All the hair-touching and the false laughter. How can't men see straight through all that, Peggy? They surely can't believe they're really that amusing.

PEGGY. Finally his favourite. Sayonara, Stalker's Joy.

ANNAG. The chap in the bowler hat seemed quite interested but the others have prised him away. They're getting a right shift on now.

MACRAE, FERGUSON *and* QUIBLICK *are almost at the post office.*

Hurry up, Peggy – they're almost here...

Coming back from having finished her task, PEGGY *is woozy on the fumes.*

PEGGY. I feel quite funny, Annag. But it's not unpleasant. Shtand still and let me look at you. Are we besht frens inshpite of the shins of our farters?

ANNAG. You cannot seem drunk, Peggy – it'll arouse suspicion.

PEGGY. That'sh a ver good point. We don't want to awry shushpishon. I have to shay, Annag, I am very shleepy.

ANNAG *props* PEGGY *against something.*

ANNAG. Try to stay upright, Peggy, and don't speak unless you're spoken to.

MACRAE, FERGUSON *and* QUIBLICK *approach.* PEGGY *waves to them.*

PEGGY. Who are all theesh piple?

ANNAG. Concentrate, Peggy.

PEGGY. Aye, aye. (*To* QUIBLICK.) Aye, aye, Captain!

MACRAE (*gesturing towards* QUIBLICK). This is the Head of the Security Intelligence Corps.

QUIBLICK. Ah. What have we here, men?

FERGUSON. Nothing we need concern ourselves with, Major.

MACRAE. I'll second that. I hope you are well, Miss Macroon.

FERGUSON. Miss Macroon runs the post office, Major. Her father Joseph is the leading merchant of Kiltod and a dear friend... to the whole community.

MACRAE. I can vouch for Macroon, too, Major. A veritable pillar. Spotless reputation. We've no cause to linger here a further moment.

QUIBLICK *is being bamboozled by his senses. He's almost certain he can smell whisky – which excites him – but at the same time he is increasingly intrigued and beguiled by the idea of* ANNAG. ANNAG *quickly realises that to distract* QUIBLICK *away from following his nose she will need to employ the same shameless techniques she has just found questionable in Murdina McCartney.*

ANNAG. Quibalick, is it, Major? I've heard that name before somewhere.

QUIBLICK *embarks on a thorough topographic survey, circling* ANNAG *admiringly.*

QUIBLICK. And you must be the fabled Annag. Your reputation precedes you, my dear.

ANNAG. Is it a compliment you're attempting, Major Quibalick?

QUIBLICK. Well you'd certainly be the talk of the town, my dear – should these islands ever contain a settlement worthy of that appellation.

FERGUSON *has noticed that* PEGGY *is about to fall asleep and possibly topple over. He claps his hands, causing her to come to suddenly.*

FERGUSON. Miss Macroon! Your father's well, I hope?

PEGGY (*having anticipated a different question*). Edinburgh.

ANNAG. Mr Macroon is away on business. No doubt he'll be sorry he missed you.

PEGGY. No doubt he'll be sorry, aye.

FERGUSON (*anxious to leave*). Well, please remember Constable Macrae and myself to him upon his return. And I think that concludes our business on Little Todday, Major.

MACRAE. I'll second that, aye. Shall we away to our... vessel, sir?

QUIBLICK. I suppose we must. Well, thank you for your time, ladies.

ANNAG. Our pleasure, I'm sure. (*Nudges* PEGGY.)

PEGGY. You're moshe welcome, Quibbley.

ANNAG. Let's get you indoors.

ANNAG *ushers* PEGGY *away.*

FERGUSON, QUIBLICK *and* MACRAE *gather for a quick post-mortem before they start out across the Coolish.*

QUIBLICK. It's a great pity we didn't turn up any stolen whisky, Mr Ferguson.

MACRAE. Perhaps you'd both like to come back to the station for a spell before heading off? There may be a wee dram in the offing. Plus I've a few cases that need shifting. We could come to an arrangement, if you follow my meaning...

QUIBLICK *is easily able to catch his meaning. They shake hands.*

QUIBLICK. Jolly good show...

MACRAE. I'll get to the boat. (*Exits.*)

QUIBLICK. Funny, it was almost as if I could smell it at times. We'd have had to confiscate it, of course. Still, saved ourselves a good deal of paperwork, I suppose.

FERGUSON. I believe our little excursion will have served as a warning, at least. Not much more we can do.

QUIBLICK. I suppose protocol dictates we really oughta rendezvous with Waggett, before close of play.

WAGGETT (BEA) *emerges, eager for his scene with* QUIBLICK.

FERGUSON. Are you sure, Major? We've had an amusing enough day thus far, I fear even a moment with Mr Waggett could only dampen the mood.

QUIBLICK. D'you know, Mr Ferguson – I believe you're right. Hang it, let the chap stew.

WAGGETT *retreats, dejected.*

FLORA *has become* MONTY *again.*

MONTY. Our investigative trio left Little Todday having failed to turn up even one case of contraband. Between them they neglected to notice how peat-stacks seemed a little larger than usual for this time of year, and how swollen ricks suggested cattle had eaten less this winter. They didn't spot where turf recently disturbed had been trodden level; or loose floorboards freshly nailed down. It also seems remarkable, in a world abundant with such innovative hidey-holes, that the great merchant Joseph Macroon should invest all his trust in a shed...

Outside Kiltod Post Office/The Harbour at Kiltod

JOSEPH (DORIS) *goes towards his shed*. PEGGY *enters and waits in dread*. JOSEPH *gives an anguished cry then removes his red hat and clutches it to his chest.*

JOSEPH. What happened here, Peggy?! What happened here?!

PEGGY. Now don't take on so…

JOSEPH. Who's after throwing away all my whisky? What creature, lassie, what creature on God's green earth could break a person's heart through such a deed?

PEGGY. Oh, Father, I confess. I'm so sorry, it was me.

JOSEPH. My own daughter could do such a thing?

PEGGY. I took a call from Snorvig yesterday. They were coming here to search. The excise, the army and the polis. They were all over the island – I was afeared they'd find your hoard.

JOSEPH. Could you not simply hide my pride and joy?

PEGGY. How could I be hiding so much? It nearly killed me opening all those cases and pouring it away. Heaven knows how much there was. It seemed to last forever.

JOSEPH. Aye, and I'd hoped it would! Eighteen cases, girl. Two hundred and sixteen bottles, and forty-eight my favourite – Stalker's Joy. Daughters? Ochòin, mo thruaighe![15] They're a misery and a burden to a man!

PEGGY (*tearful*). I'm sure, Father, I only did it for the best.

JOSEPH. Your poor late mother would never have done such a fool of a thing for the best. She'd more sense. What a world it is where a daughter's whim wastes a whisky windfall. You weigh a man down, girl, you weigh a man down!

PEGGY (*gathering herself*). I'm sure I don't wish to be a burden, father. Say the word and Fred and me can be married in Easter week, and that'll be one foolish daughter out of your hair!

15. *Ochòin, mo thruaighe* [ochone, mo roo-y] – Alas, my grief.

JOSEPH. Aye, and I'd sooner see you married, girl, than at large
to pour away more of my treasure. I'll get over you leaving,
lass – but I'll never cease to mourn my Stalker's Joy.

Colourful bunting and flags appear as MONTY *steps
forward…*

MONTY. And so on April 11th the banns of marriage between
Alfred Ernest Odd and Peggy Elizabeth Macroon were read
and later that month the first of three weddings that year on
the islands went full steam ahead. Flags waved in the gentle
breeze. The whimbrels in the distance cried that May was
almost here.

Who's Perce?

Everywhere were wheatears…

Who's Perce?

…and stonechats…

Who's Perce?

…eager to add their various voices to the air of celebration.
All agreed it was a golden afternoon.

DUNCAN (JULIET) *enters to begin his ballad. This can be
sung a cappella, or with accompaniment, or simply recited
as a dramatic poem. As the ballad progresses the cast
appear:* FRED (CONNIE) *with a nosegay of daisies in his
uniform;* JOSEPH (DORIS); PEGGY (AILEEN, *as soon as
she's ready*) – *in a long white lace blusher wedding veil;*
FATHER MACALISTER (FLORA), *well-oiled and in his
element; dapper* DOCTOR MACLAREN (WIN); *and*
ANNAG NO. 1 (BEA).

DUNCAN *delivers 'Ode to an Odd Couple'…*

O he was the stranger who sailed to our island
And she was the beauty who captured his heart
O he was a soldier and she was a maiden
And there could be nothing to keep them apart.

He is fine, he is handsome – Fred's worth a king's ransom
As his milit'ry pension heaves into sight

And time shall not wither a well-furnished quiver
Nor age serve to dampen a knight's appetite.

With lips like the rowan and dark hair a-flowin'
And bright eyes a-glinting and glowing with health
She is brave, she is bonnie, Peg's smart and she's funny
Had I the gumption I'd've wooed her myself.

So praise be to Eros and to Aphrodite
And praise be to Venus and Cupid and Pan
And blessèd be Bacchus, who we've all felt the lack of
Here's to this odd couple – our Peg and her man.

When the ballad ends, FATHER MACALISTER *leads the applause.*

FATHER MACALISTER. A golden lad, I think we'll all agree. Bard, thou thy wordy task hast done. You'll require a small sensation. What have you there, Joseph?

JOSEPH. White Label, Father. Duty paid.

FATHER MACALISTER. Did you get this from Roderick MacRurie, Joseph?

The bottle is handed to DUNCAN.

JOSEPH. I did, Father.

FATHER MACALISTER. By jingo, you're the great diplomat, Joseph. Now, speak up, man. Silence for the father of the bride!

JOSEPH addresses the guests – and the audience. DUNCAN *can leave during or after the speech.*

JOSEPH. Unlike my friend and fellow clansman, Duncan Macroon, I have few words, and most of them short. We've had our differences, but Peggy's a great girl and a good daughter. And she'll make a grand companion for Sergeant Odd, so long as he remembers that it's a foolish man reckons himself smarter than his wife. Let's drink their health in this beautiful whisky which arrived in the very nick of time. Slàinte mhath!

ALL. Slàinte mhath!

DOCTOR MACLAREN *talks to* ANNAG.

DOCTOR MACLAREN. So, Annag, when do you suppose you'll be setting yourself up to make some fellow's life a living hell?

ANNAG. Och, indeed, I don't know, doctor – I believe I'll soon be on the shelf.

DOCTOR MACLAREN. Come now, Annag, there's not a woman on these islands can turn heads the way you do.

ANNAG. I could turn all the heads in the world, doctor, but it'd mean nothing so long as the one I want to notice me never looks my way.

DOCTOR MACLAREN. In my medical opinion, Annag, there's not a man on these two islands hasn't looked your way.

ANNAG. And are you talking now as a doctor, doctor?

DOCTOR MACLAREN. No, Annag – I'm talking as a man.

ANNAG. Then I hope later you'll do the decent thing, and ask a girl to dance.

PEGGY *notices* ANNAG *touch* DOCTOR MACLAREN*'s face, then exit. Now* FATHER MACALISTER *takes command of the room.*

FATHER MACALISTER. Now I'd just like to speak up for the Sergeant, if I may, Joseph. In the Old West, a place I am pleased to visit often in my imagination – a place where men were men and women were not – a fellow of good character would be known as 'a man to ride the river with'. The Sergeant, in my opinion, sizes up to being such a man. The only black mark against him that I can find is that he's not a Scot – but that can't be helped I suppose; perhaps he ought not feel too much cast down by the failure of his forebears. Let the Sergeant speak!

FRED *rises, uncertainly.*

FRED. Father Macalister and all friends, I thank you very much for the kind way in which you have drunk the health of Peggy and... er... myself. I took a fancy to Little Todday the moment I set foot on it nearly two years ago and I think I maybe realised I was to find here the girl I'd been looking for all my life. You'll hear a lot of people say there's no such a thing as love at first sight; I know there is. I'm the luckiest man there ever was.

PEGGY *kisses* FRED. WAGGETT (BEA) *and* DOLLY (JULIET) *have entered.*

FATHER MACALISTER. So having concluded the speeches, we are all free to enjoy ourselves as best as we see fit. Within reasonable limitations, of course.

WAGGETT. Excuse me, Father Macalister, but I should like to say a few words.

FATHER MACALISTER. Certainly, Colonel, the stage is yours.

WAGGETT. I don't know why Father Macalister gives me a rank to which I'm not entitled, I am a simple captain.

FATHER MACALISTER. By my soul, a swain, a most simple clown.

WAGGETT. Doubtless we all wish to express our grateful thanks to Mr Joseph Macroon for his hospitality. But I hope none of you will take it amiss if I now utter a word of warning. Everyone here knows that *The Cabinet Minister* has been wrecked and that the greater part of her cargo consists of whisky. (*Cheers.*) That whisky, I would remind you, is government property; it does not belong to you...

DOCTOR MACLAREN *steps in.*

DOCTOR MACLAREN. I'm going to have to interrupt you, I'm afraid, Mr Waggett. I think we'd all be relieved to return to the reason we're here, which is to toast the future happiness of Peggy and Fred. Your most unwelcome intervention has put a damper on proceedings. This isn't the occasion for half-baked, patronising lectures, as any intelligent person would know.

WAGGETT. Are you implying, Doctor Maclaren, that I am deficient in sense?

DOCTOR MACLAREN. It need not be implied, Mr Waggett, it is taken as given.

WAGGETT. I've half a mind to ask you to step outside, Doctor Maclaren.

DOCTOR MACLAREN. You've half a mind, Captain, we can all agree to that.

FATHER MACALISTER. Enough! In spite of the government, who in my opinion should look after their own affairs and keep their noses out of ours, we shall raise our glasses to Sergeant Major Odd and Peggy his bride! (*Drains his glass.*) Will you join me for some air, doctor, Joseph?

DOCTOR MACLAREN. Fresh air, Father, would be pleasant, aye.

JOSEPH, DOCTOR MACLAREN *and* FATHER MACALISTER *exit.* FRED *approaches* WAGGETT *and* DOLLY.

FRED. Mrs Waggett, you look spectacular. I fear Peggy will imagine you seek to upstage her. I'm glad you could make it, sir. Doctor Maclaren is rather in his element, I'm afraid.

DOLLY. I did warn my husband that today might be a good day to avoid mention of Minnie.

WAGGETT. The Catholics do like to make an awful fuss, of course, when it comes to this sort of thing. No offence intended, Sergeant Major.

FRED. I'm happy to go along with it all, sir. We military men are used to contending with protocol, are we not? A little more won't kill us, I suppose.

DOLLY. I don't think it's a fuss, Paul, I think these things matter. After all, people only get married once. Well, I mean, nice people do. (*Thinks.*) Unless... there's a terrible accident, of course...

THE BIFFER (FLORA), DROOBY (AILEEN) *and*
DONALD (WIN) *arrive*.

FRED. Quite… Well… here's The Biffer and Drooby and
Donald. If you'll excuse me…

   FRED *goes to greet them*. WAGGETT *and* DOLLY *exit*.

   I hadn't hoped to see you, lads – what with everything else
   going on.

DONALD. We can't stop long, Sergeant, but we wanted to look
in. I've said I'd be helping the boys here with a little bit of a
removals job.

DROOBY (*grabbing a drink and taking a hefty swig*). Well,
I don't mind having just a swift one, Sergeant, to wet the
baby's head.

THE BIFFER. You'll excuse my friend, Sergeant, if he's a trifle
premature.

DROOBY. Mature, aye. I'll say this for your new people,
Sergeant, they were good to us that first night we went out to
fetch the Minnie.

THE BIFFER. Though the Minnie is not a thing to be mentioning
to big Roderick, of course. He's still a wee bit raw.

DONALD. Was he sending Annag to your shindig as a
representative, did we hear?

FRED. Annag was about, earlier, yes. I think I saw her
carousing Doc Maclaren.

DONALD. I'll go and find him. (*Has a leg spasm.*) I think
I need a word… (*Limps off.*)

THE BIFFER. Annag's a fine girl. At times I'd say her
pulchritude is almost transcendental.

DROOBY. Dental, aye. And the doc's a grand fella. For all he
drinks, his hand is ever steady.

THE BIFFER. But we mustn't impose on your hospitality any
further, Sergeant.

CATRIONA (DORIS) *is approaching*.

DROOBY. Is it Miss Macleod did the buffet? We'll pick something up on our way out, just to be polite.

THE BIFFER *and* DROOBY *exit*.

FRED. Help yourself, boys. Catriona. I haven't thanked you properly for that marvellous spread. No one would suspect there's a war on.

CATRIONA. George is a dab hand with the shotgun, it turns out. Due to Home Guard shooting practice, I assume.

FRED. George was always a natural. But a bit of confidence helps, I'm sure. I understand you've plumped for a quiet wedding on the mainland?

CATRIONA. Yes, that's partly George not wanting to be the centre of attention, of course, plus it won't be much fun without Norman. He's still hoping the RAF will give him leave to come to Glasgow but says we mustn't get our hopes up.

DOCTOR MACLAREN (WIN) *enters*.

DOCTOR MACLAREN. I was just saying to George, Catriona – if I weren't the only doctor in the two islands I'd come to Glasgow and give you away myself.

CATRIONA. And you'd be the perfect substitute, doctor. Congratulations, Peggy!

PEGGY (AILEEN) *has joined them. She hands the bouquet to* CATRIONA.

PEGGY. You're next.

DOCTOR MACLAREN. Always the bridesmaid, never the bride – that's my lot in life, Mrs Odd.

PEGGY. Well, I don't know about that, doctor. I'd say you and Annag MacRurie looked thick as thieves earlier.

CATRIONA. For sure Annag'd make any man a lovely wife, doctor.

DUNCAN (JULIET) *enters, with* FATHER MACALISTER (FLORA).

DOCTOR MACLAREN. Ach, get away with you. I'm too old a hand to be caught now. The bard and I were born to be bachelors. Is that not right, young man?

DUNCAN. Never say never, Doctor. I'm sure George Campbell never thought he'd be anything but a bachelor for the rest of his days.

CATRIONA. And that would still be so, had his mother had her way.

FRED. We ought also to give thanks to 'St Minnie', as Father Macalister calls it.

DOCTOR MACLAREN. If you'll permit me to proffer a medical opinion, I'd say there's very little in life that can't be improved by what that great coiner of phrases Father Mac calls 'a small sensation'.

FATHER MACALISTER. Let's drink to that, then. A future improved by small sensations.

ALL. Slàinte mhath!

ANNAG NO. 1 (BEA) *enters*.

ANNAG. Wait for me. Doctor Maclaren? I believe you promised me a dance.

FATHER MACALISTER. We'll need a song, from our bard, to celebrate our bountiful blessings.

DUNCAN *starts to sing 'Bard's Bounty'. All join in.*
DOCTOR MACLAREN *and* ANNAG *dance*.

ALL. Bonnie Doon, Highland Heart, Prince's Choice, Mountain Tarn,
Fiona's Farewell, Salmon's Leap, Lammermoor...
Northern Light, Stalker's Joy and Over the Border,
O Whisky a gogo, O Whisky galore!

King's Own, Scottish Envoy, Chief's Choice, Silver Whistle,
Road to the Isles, Thistle Cream, Albadhor...

Bluebell, Annie Laurie and Tartan Perfection,
O Whisky a gogo, O Whisky galore!

Auld Stuarts, High Heather, Pipe Major, Glen Gloaming,
All the Year Round, Fingal's Cave, Bannachmore...
Stag's Breath, Lion Rampant and Queen of the Islands
O Whisky a gogo, O Whisky galore!

The End.

*The first curtain call is as the Pallas Players. The company
single out* JULIET. *The second curtain call is as themselves.*

Character Descriptions

Obviously the basic descriptions below, drawn from the information available, serve only as a rough guide. It is impossible to expect the 'seven threadbare women' of the Pallas Players to reproduce accurate facsimiles of the various characters they seek to inhabit. The aim, therefore, is to capture a convincing essence. Peggy need not be dark-haired, though Monty will still describe her as such. The original producers decided against the excessive spitting or snuff-taking mentioned in the novel – so despite these skills being proudly asterisked on the résumés of certain performers, their proficiency in those areas remained untested.

FLORA BELLERBY plays:

MONTY   Accent – English. Authoritative. Theatrical. Based on Compton Mackenzie. 'Monty', as he was always known to his friends, was born into a family that operated its own touring theatre company. He was said to be rather 'theatrical' himself: 'Marching around his domain in a kilt and sporran, nobody looked more like a Highland chief.' But Monty wasn't born a Scot, and he didn't sound like a Scot – his paternal ancestors left Scotland in the eighteenth century. He was sixty-three when he wrote the novel, and seventy-two when our play is set.

THE BIFFER   Accent – Scots. Confident. Clear. He enjoys the sound of his own voice. He is Archie MacRurie, but prefers to be known as 'The Biffer'. He is a fisherman of prowess about fifty years old. His nickname (according to a previous book) comes from his extraordinary success in the boxing ring when he was a young man. He owns a boat called the *Kittiwake*. In the play he is quite loquacious, inspired by Monty's real-life friend 'The Coddie', who was an expert raconteur. Monty wrote that The Coddie had 'a fine feeling for language. Not only for his native Gaelic, but even for our English, which he speaks like a king.'

FATHER MACALISTER   Accent– Scots. Rich. Warm. Deep.
'"Great sticks alive, Sergeant, welcome back to Paradise," the
priest exclaimed in that rich voice whose warm vibrato had
made so many feel truly welcome to his hearth.' He has a
profound bass, a booming response and a magnificent guffaw.
He enjoys pulp Western novels.

CONSTABLE MACRAE   Accent – Scots. From Kintail, in
the north-west Highlands. He is lazy and extremely corruptible
and 'would not do a thing unless he was asked to'. He is not a
fan of Waggett, because Waggett would question Macrae's
ability to do his job properly. Macrae believes rules and
regulations are mostly created by people with not enough to do,
to give other people with not enough to do reason to keep busy.
His easy-going attitude means that anybody not having to have
professional dealings with him would find him rather genial.

CONNIE CALVERT plays:

FRED ODD   Accent – English. Born in London but brought
up in Nottingham. Forty-five years old. Sergeant Major Alfred
Odd has a 'twinkle in his eye'. One married female character
says to him, after he compliments her on her 'spirit': 'Get along
with you, Sergeant. We never had to teach you the blarney. You
had enough for yourself, even if you are a Sassunnach.' Nearly
everybody likes Fred. He's charming.

MAJOR QUIBLICK   Accent – English. Posh. Major P St
John Quiblick is 'a man with the expression of a professional
palmist, who had become a major so recently that he was still as
proud of his crown as a king.' To the islanders, he is 'just a
clown'. In an earlier book he was described as smiling 'the
weary smile of one who has plumbed too often the uttermost
depths of human deception'.

ANNAG No. 3   Accent – Scots. From Great Todday. Her
father Roderick owns The Snorvig Hotel and Bar, where Annag
works. Boggust observes to himself that she is 'really rather a
pretty girl'. Annag's 'look' may be influenced by Lana Turner in
Slightly Dangerous. Soon to be twenty-one, she carries a torch

for Doctor Maclaren, though he seems unaware of this. Annag is pronounced Annack (AH-nak).

CAPTAIN HEADLEY FAVERSHAM   Accent – English. West Country. Captain of *The Cabinet Minister*. He is called Buncher in the novel, and has 'a small grizzled beard, a high complexion and hair as dark as the rock on which his ship had struck.' Mackenzie doesn't give us much to go on, but extensive research reveals that Captain Beaconsfield Worthington of the SS *Politician*, the wrecked ship which inspired *Whisky Galore*, was 'a stolid but not entirely humourless sixty-three-year-old man from Plymouth in the West Country of England.'

WIN HEWITT plays:

DONALD MacKECHNIE   Accent – Scots. Captain of *The Island Queen*. In a previous novel we learn that: 'The voice of Captain MacKechnie was high-pitched at any time. When he grew angry the pitch of his voice sharpened... and trembled upon the air like the rarefied squeak of an infuriated bat.'

DR MACLAREN   Accent – Scots. From Great Todday. Studied at Glasgow University. A 'jovial, hard-drinking, and thoroughly competent medical man.' His 'usually jovial florid face was lined with bad temper. He was a man who liked his dram and he was beginning to feel the effects of no whisky on himself.' He likes snuff, fine wine and good food.

MRS CAMPBELL   Accent – Scots. Originally from Mull. Seventy-five years old. 'A majestic old woman, with icy pale blue eyes and a deep husky voice.' Critical of everybody – she vehemently opposes the consumption of alcohol. She would pronounce the word modern as 'modderrrn' with the scornful rolling of the 'r'. 'She had produced her only offspring late in life and still regarded him as a child of ten in spite of the fact that he was thirty-five years old and a headmaster.' She is a bigoted, fossilised terror. In the novel Fred says he'd 'sooner be up against one Hitler than a world full of Mrs Campbells.'

ANNAG NO. 2   See under Connie.

TOM FERGUSON   Accent – Scots. From Aberdeen. The
Exciseman at Nobost. 'A sharp-nosed little man in a suit of
Glenurquhart tweed, with the sing-song accent of Aberdeen.'
According to Donald he's: 'One of these wise men of the East.
He thinks himself pretty smart. Och, but he's not a bad fellow at
all.'

PADDY NO. 3   A Dog. 'Captain Waggett's overgrown Irish
Setter that was more like an auburn-haired St Bernard.'

DORIS SANDERSON plays:

JOSEPH MACROON   Accent – Scots. From Little Todday.
Aged sixty-three. The postmaster and leading merchant and
Chief Warden (air raid) of Kiltod. He always wears 'his knitted
red cap' and a greatcoat. Smokes a pipe with deep gurgling
puffs. Spits tobacco juice after gurgling. Owns a motorboat
called *The Morning Star*. In a previous book he is described as
'a sharp-featured man with a trim grey moustache, quick in his
movements, who always wore a knitted red cap such as trolls
wear in illustrated fairytales.'

CATRIONA MACLEOD   Accent – Scots. From Great
Todday. She is 'pretty' and 'a splendid cook'. She is 'for an
Islander an economical housekeeper'. She has 'deft housewifely
fingers', 'quick movements', and 'sparkling warmth' in her
'bright, dark-brown eyes'. That all sounds a bit much, but those
are the impressions of the man who loves her to distraction.
According to other characters 'she's one of the nicest girls on
the island' and 'There isn't a better cook in Todaidh Mòr.'
Catriona is smart and feisty and confident and determined.

RODERICK MacRURIE   Accent – Scots. From Great
Todday. The owner of The Snorvig Hotel and Bar. Possessing of
'great bulk', Roderick has, according to a previous book: 'dark
eyes under black-tufted eyebrows.'

PADDY NO. 2   See under Win.

AILEEN McCORMACK plays:

DROOBY   Accent – Scots. From Great Todday. He is really Alan Galbraith, but 'is always known as Drooby, a nickname the origin of which none could tell except Drooby himself, and he never would.' Drooby wishes he was as good with words as The Biffer, who he admires greatly.

PEGGY MACROON   Accent – Scots. From Little Todday. Joseph's daughter and Fred's girlfriend. Aged twenty-five. A 'most attractive girl', with 'deep-blue slanting eyes' and 'dark brown hair'. She runs the post office on Little Todday.

GEORGE CAMPBELL   Accent – Scots. From Great Todday. Thirty-five years old. A 'small shy man who, until the formation of the Home Guard, had scarcely ever been seen in public'. He is dominated by his ferocious mother.

PADDY NO. 1   See under Win.

LIEUTENANT BOGGUST AKA MR BROWN   Accent – English. This 'young man with a neo-Caroline moustache' is based with the Security Intelligence Corps at Nobost, Mid-Uist. 'If his nose had been a little shorter and his chin a little longer he would not have been bad-looking. He was sporting plus-fours of the barrage-balloon type, from the umber convolutions of which his ankles emerged like chicken-bones.' He overestimates his abilities, including his mastery of disguise; his undercover operation as a 'tweed merchant' fails due to his woeful lack of research into the tweed industry, but also to his underestimation of the intelligence of the locals. He is described as 'just a jessie' by one of the islanders.

BEA CORNFORD plays:

PAUL WAGGETT   Accent – English. Fifties. Seems posh. Sold out from his partnership in a firm of London chartered accountants and retired to Great Todday before the outbreak of WWII. Drives a 'veteran 16 hp Austin'. He rents the shooting of the two islands from the Department of Agriculture. Captain Waggett commands the Home Guard and enjoys reading action-packed Crime Club yarns. Sees himself as straight-talking and longs to be respected by the islanders, who will only ever regard him as an imbecile. 'Of course, if the people would listen more to what I tell them, I could be of even more use; but they're very unresponsive to new ideas, except of course the claptrap talked by these Labour fellows. They're responsive enough to that.' He was one of the inspirations for Captain Mainwaring in Dad's Army.

ANNAG NO. 1   See under Connie.

ROBBIE BAIRD   Accent – Scots. Clydeside. Chief Officer on *The Cabinet Minister*. Red hair. In the novel he's simply a seaman, but we needed to get the Captain ashore, so it seemed to make more sense that the Captain would volunteer his second-in-command to accompany him to the island, leaving his third-in-command in charge of the crew – who are already off the ship and waiting in the lifeboats.

JULIET MAINWARING plays:

DOLLY WAGGETT   Accent – English. Aged forties. Married to Paul Waggett (former London chartered accountant) for twenty-five years. Long-suffering, underappreciated by her husband, perhaps a frustrated romantic. 'She was looking a little more like a battered nursery doll than usual.' She has a soft spot for Fred.

NORMAN MACLEOD   Accent – Scots. From Great Todday. 'The attractive young schoolmaster of Watasett.' He is an expert poacher and a socialist, or, according to Mrs Campbell: 'a good-for-nothing radical'. He is an enthusiast for the powers of whisky and remains a confirmed bachelor. He has 'postponed the notion of marriage altogether. Cupid rhymes with stupid for me.' He joins the RAF and goes off to serve.

DUNCAN MACROON   Accent – Scots. From Little Todday. Duncan is a poet and a crofter and has 'fair tumbled hair and glowing countenance and eyes as blue as the kingfisher's wing.' He was a promising student at Glasgow University until a girlfriend jilted him. He returned to a solitary life on the croft he inherited along with £2,000, the income from which allows him to indulge in bouts of deep drinking, when one neighbour or another will look after his cows and fowls until he has recovered. Never publishes, despite offers from publishers, as the poems are never finished to his satisfaction.

ANNAG NO. 4   See under Connie.

Whisky Galore: Ode to an Odd Couple

a capella version

Philip Goulding

Alan Edward Williams

health   She's brave and she's bon ny, Peg's smart and she's fun-ny and   had I the

gump-tion I'd have woo'd her my - self_____   so   praise be to   E - ros and

to Aph - ro - di - te and_ praise be to Ve-nus and Cu-pid and Pan,_____   and_

bless - ed   be   Bacc - us who we've all felt   the   lack of, here's to this   odd

coup - le   our Peg   and her   man_____

Whisky Galore: Ode to an Odd Couple

piano version

Philip Goulding

Alan Edward Williams

Whisky Galore: Bard's Bounty
lead sheet

Philip Goulding

Alan Edward Williams

Lively

Bon nie Doon, High - land Heart, Princ-e's Choice, Mount - ain Tarn,___ Fi - on - a's Fare

well, Salm-on's Leap, Lamm - er moor........... North-ern Light, Stal - ker's Joy,___ and

O - ver the Bor - der, O Whis-ky a - go - go, O Whis - ky Ga - lore_____

King's Own, Scott - ish Env - oy, Chief's Choice, Sil - ver Whist - le,___ Road to the

King's Own, Scott - ish Env - oy, Chief's Choice, Sil - ver Whist - le, Road to the

Isles, Thist le Cream, Al - bad - hor_____ Blue-bell, An-nie Laur-ie and Tar-tan per

Isles, Thist - le Cream Al- bad - hor_____ Blue-bell, An-nie Laur-ie and Tar-tan per

2

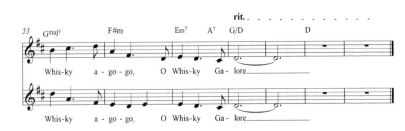

Whisky Galore: Bard's Bounty

Philip Goulding

piano version

Alan Edward Williams

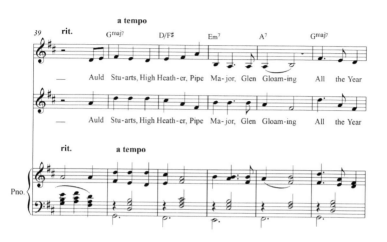

Other Adaptations in this Series

ANIMAL FARM
Ian Wooldridge
Adapted from George Orwell

ANNA KARENINA
Helen Edmundson
Adapted from Leo Tolstoy

ARABIAN NIGHTS
Dominic Cooke

AROUND THE WORLD IN 80 DAYS
Laura Eason
Adapted from Jules Verne

THE CANTERBURY TALES
Mike Poulton
Adapted from Geoffrey Chaucer

A CHRISTMAS CAROL
Karen Louise Hebden
Adapted from Charles Dickens

CORAM BOY
Helen Edmundson
Adapted from Jamila Gavin

DAVID COPPERFIELD
Alastair Cording
Adapted from Charles Dickens

DIARY OF A NOBODY
Hugh Osborne
Adapted from George Grossmith
& Wheedon Grossmith

DR JEKYLL AND MR HYDE
David Edgar
Adapted from Robert Louis Stevenson

DRACULA: THE BLOODY TRUTH
Le Navet Bete & John Nicholson
Adapted from Bram Stoker

EMMA
Martin Millar and Doon MacKichan
Adapted from Jane Austen

FRANKENSTEIN
Patrick Sandford
Adapted from Mary Shelley

GREAT EXPECTATIONS
Nick Ormerod and Declan Donnellan
Adapted from Charles Dickens

THE HAUNTING
Hugh Janes
Adapted from Charles Dickens

HIS DARK MATERIALS
Nicholas Wright
Adapted from Philip Pullman

THE HOUND OF
THE BASKERVILLES
Steven Canny & John Nicholson
Adapted from Arthur Conan Doyle

JANE EYRE
Polly Teale
Adapted from Charlotte Brontë

JEEVES AND WOOSTER IN
PERFECT NONSENSE
The Goodale Brothers
Adapted from P.G. Wodehouse

THE JUNGLE BOOK
Stuart Paterson
Adapted from Rudyard Kipling

KENSUKE'S KINGDOM
Stuart Paterson
Adapted from Michael Morpurgo

KES
Lawrence Till
Adapted from Barry Hines

THE MASSIVE TRAGEDY
OF MADAME BOVARY
John Nicholson & Javier Marzan
Adapted from Gustave Flaubert

THE RAGGED TROUSERED
PHILANTHROPISTS
Howard Brenton
Adapted from Robert Tressell

THE RAILWAY CHILDREN
Mike Kenny
Adapted from E. Nesbit

SWALLOWS AND AMAZONS
Helen Edmundson and Neil Hannon
Adapted from Arthur Ransome

THE THREE MUSKETEERS
John Nicholson & Le Navet Bete
Adapted from Alexander Dumas

TREASURE ISLAND
Stuart Paterson
Adapted from Robert Louis Stevenson

THE WIND IN THE WILLOWS
Mike Kenny
Adapted from Kenneth Grahame